D1088386

THE LONDONER'S ENGLAND

THE
LONDONER'S
ENGLAND

CONTEMPORARY WATER-COLOURS AND DRAWINGS OF
LONDON AND THE HOME COUNTIES REPRODUCED BY
COLOUR AND MONOCHROME LITHOGRAPHY & BY HALF-
TONE: ASSEMBLED & EDITED WITH DESCRIPTIVE TEXT

BY ALAN BOTT

THE MACMILLAN COMPANY
NEW YORK 1948

PRINTED IN GREAT BRITAIN

CONTENTS

LIST OF PLATES AND ARTISTS

(Plates marked with an asterisk are in colour)

vii

INDEX OF TOPOGRAPHICAL REFERENCES

I

TOPOGRAPHICAL REFERENCES

TOPOGRAPHICAL REFERENCES

ACKNOWLEDGMENTS

IN the introductory chapter that follows I have referred at some length to the public-spirited sponsors of 'The Londoner's England' Exhibition of water-colours and drawings, to which I am primarily indebted for the inception of this book. The Exhibition was organised by Sir Charles Tennyson, C.M.G., and Mr. T. A. Fennemore, respectively Chairman and Director of the Central Institute of Art and Design, and the members of the Selection Committee were Sir Kenneth Clark, K.C.B., Sir William Russell Flint, R.A., and Professor P. H. Jowett, R.W.S. (Chairman).

For permission to reproduce pictures which were not in that Exhibition acknowledgment is made to the artists concerned, and to the following owners of pictures: Mrs. W. A. Younger for *Constitution Hill* by Henry Rushbury, R.A.; Mr. C. Dalton for *The Campus, Welwyn Garden City* by A. R. Whitear; Messrs. Roland, Browse and Delbanco for *Cheyne Row* by Clifford Hall; Messrs. Heal and Son, Co. Ltd., for *Staple Inn* by Tom Waghorn, *St. Paul's from Bankside* by the late S. Dennant Moss, and *Fisher Street, Lewes* by Dorothy Watts; the Fine Art Society Ltd. for *The Monument* by Kenneth Steel; and Mr. Raymond Smith, Librarian of the Guildhall Library, for *The Guildhall* by Sydney R. Jones.

In the compilation of the book valuable assistance has been courteously given by a number of people, among whom the following should be specially mentioned: Mr. A. D. Forshaw; Mr. A. G. Thompson of the Port of London Authority (author of various well-known books on London River); Mr. E. J. Gibbons of the Thames Conservancy; Miss Eileen Smith; Mr. R. F. Bavington Jones; Mr. H. V. Harley; Mr. David Keswick; the Rev. B. J. Corder; the Rev. R. Routh; the Rev. F. C. Baker; Mr. J. G. Ward; Mr. Kenneth Saville; Mr. C. Tuke-Taylor; Sir Metford Watkins; Mr. Adrian Bury; and the Head Vergers of St. Paul's Cathedral and Westminster Abbey. Sincere thanks are also due to many Town Clerks, Public Librarians, rectors and vicars, antiquarians, hoteliers, lock-keepers and occupiers of historic houses; and to the author and publishers (Messrs. Macmillan & Company, Ltd.), for permission to print the extract from Mr. Ralph Hodgson's *Poems*, which is quoted on page 16.

A. B.

SOMETHING ABOUT LONDON

LONDON has been called many things: a hell by Shelley, a monster by Cobbett, a kindly nurse by Tennyson, a nation by Disraeli, the flower of cities all (' gemme of all joy, jasper of jocunditie ') by William Dunbar. Each of the apostrophes has a touch of truth. London has for so long been so vast a fact that since the Middle Ages no Englishmen anywhere in the world, few Scotsmen and Welshmen (or indeed, men of North France and the Low Countries) have been outside its influence. It is too many-sided to be seen whole: much of the image comes from the beholder's temperament.

Shelley at one extreme, Cobbett at another, were unfitted to like London; whereas Tennyson was in poetic tune with it, and Disraeli adored solid grandeur. As for William Dunbar, writing his verse in a City swelling to its own prosperity, the vigour of the young Henry VIII and the Renaissance winds from France and Italy, he was no doubt one of those who love London more than their racial North: one of the multitude who, in every century since Bannockburn, insistently sigh for Scotland but as insistently choose London. No other capital city has adopted so many loyal but particularised citizens as the swarms of London Scots who allot one day a year to clannish dinners, two or three more to inter-racial football and the rest to life as lived by born Londoners. There are no such sentimental bandings among Paris Gascons and Berlin Bavarians; some become Parisians or Berliners, most remain unchanged Gascon or Bavarian.

London is an unlimited Adoption Society. For centuries, none except the little minority born less than a mile from Bow Church has believed that the test of citizenship is to be born within sound of Bow Bells. Ever since the Church lost its City manors and Tudor London overflowed to absorb Southwark and Westminster, that ancient tale has been as much a myth as the wise cat and early poverty of Sir Richard Whittington, a Lord Mayor who was born with a Guild-marked silver spoon in his mouth. What, then, is a Londoner? Anybody who, born no matter where, has acquired so strong a taste for London that it out-flavours all other cities. He may retire to the country or a quiet place in another land, but he keeps always the image of London, or some part of London: it may be anywhere between Highgate Hill and Peckham Rye. For him, Piccadilly Circus is in fact the Centre of the World. Back on a visit, he is at one with the crowds and the smell of wet pavements.

5

Absent, he will stop before any picture, print or etching (the more exact, architectural warts and all, the more it will please him) of any house-row that recalls London.

A Londoner by adoption may not recognise the flavour until, having left London for long enough, he acquires a nostalgia that persists till death. It assembles itself gradually, from details of experience that grow sharper with memory. I was no Londoner in the year when, pitchforked into the big city from an abruptly truncated period of college on the Continent, I found work on the news agency then directed by Baron de Reuter in Old Jewry; but the London of 1913 is for me as exact as the acutely experienced London of the 1940 bombs. In those days war in Europe seemed unthinkable except as an excitement in the Balkans. My job was to translate telegrams that arrived at night, recording events from the last of the purely Balkan wars. I knew next to nobody in London. After work and late supper I walked, whatever the weather, through some part of the City, the West End or Bloomsbury. Those walks were an apprenticeship to London, but showed nothing below the solid surface. Then, one night, I met in a café-bar somebody who took me up three flights of stairs in Greek Street, Soho, to where a crowded company were eating snacks, drinking tall steins of Pilsner and talking to beat the improvised band. It was the Crab Tree, almost the first of the neo-Georgian night-clubs for those who practised, patronised or dithered around the early twentieth-century arts. My expenditure on that ambrosial night, which ended in some Turkish Baths in Russell Square, with a group collected by Harold Monro (then establishing his Poetry Bookshop near-by), was enough to limit my supper for days to sand-wiches in Reuter's offices. As a young man's initiation fee to an aspect of London life, it was very cheap; especially as it led to a sequence of later experiences that include an odd display by Mr. Aleister Crowley in South Kensington of magical practice, and an odder expedition when the late Horace de Vere Cole led a gang of corduroyed, amateur navvies down Piccadilly, where they roped off a part of the roadway, and with picks and shovels un-hurriedly dug a large, entirely unauthorised hole, which stayed there for days before some authority thought of asking who the devil had made it (my minor rôle was to keep watch against policemen—who took no notice despite the too bright scarves of the 'navvies'—and any inquisitive onlookers who looked like being from a public works department).

These metropolitan adventures, which at the time seemed like something from the *New Arabian Nights*, revealed what every alert inhabitant of a great city discovers: that it is a peculiar place as well as an ordered one. In London there have always been byways to withdrawal from regulated citizenship. Before this book came to be planned I had studied the architectural styles of London in a desultory way, but had investigated the history of only one district. At one time in youth I was a foreign sub-editor on the old *Daily*

Chronicle; and I gave the short break from desk-work in Salisbury Square each evening to reconstruction of the Carmelite region south of the Temple. It was the local names like Hanging Sword Alley that persuaded me to read up the records of London's Alsatia for outlaws and criminals. They are comparatively few, but enough to give the story-tellers their images of a district grimy and lusty as that of François Villon in fifteenth-century Paris (only, Alsatia never had a Villon).

The most earnest Londoners are those who cherish London because of its past. From an early taste for Harrison Ainsworth they graduate to factual history, and sometimes achieve what few except scholars ever complete: a full reading of Stow's great *Survey*, from which Ainsworth and the rest of London's historical novelists drew as copiously as Shakespeare drew from Holinshed. I am not among these; I have permitted myself a degree of personal recollection because I count myself typical of the big, casual but faithful majority of Londoners by adoption. These learn something of the City's past, but do it incidentally or accidentally, after absorbing the essence of London's contemporary life and backgrounds. Away at the wars or in exile, their longing is less for the fragrant Grantchesters where they were born, than for the highways and small streets, the occasions and spectacles and, especially, the crowds and types of their metropolis. When I was abroad during the 1920's, recording the conferences and revolutions and situations that developed all over Europe, the best moment of each journey came with the exit from Victoria or from Croydon airport. I worked during part of the 1920's for Lord Northcliffe; and it was a habit of that Jovian individualist to deflate any lesser individualist whom he believed to be in danger of growing too big for his boots. My turn came when some international statesmen were in London to confer with Lloyd George. It was also the time of the Beaver craze, when young women competed with fluty young men to spot and classify the beards that passed through the streets, parks, district trains and places where they crowd. My deflation in prestige took the form of transfer from the status of By Our Diplomatic Correspondent to that of By Our Beaver Correspondent. I went to see Willy Clarkson in Wardour Street, who fitted me with a wide, brown, two-pronged beard. With this and a top-hat above a waisted overcoat, I walked the West End, frequented the railway stations and collected, for descriptions of how London had gone Beaver, the comments on my Double Emperor beard. For an unselfconscious Londoner, nothing could have been better fun or felt less like a puncture of personality.

The adventure in beards led to another of the sort that has often helped to turn young penmen from the counties (including the author of *Sketches by Boz*) into Londoners—an assignment to write articles on famous streets. Only half of the series was done when I had to leave for Lausanne, where Lord Curzon (attended by the glorious valet of whom Mr. Harold Nicolson wrote in

7

Some People), M. Poincaré, Ismet Pasha, Benito Mussolini and others were meeting to promote, for all time, peace in the Near East. But the investigation of Bond Street, the Whitechapel Road, Hammersmith's hearty King Street and the rest, had increased my taste for the topography of Town. I believed my knowledge of it to be extensive and peculiar; and when, soon afterward, I said a grateful farewell to Fleet Street (on the principle that journalism is a good thing to have been in) I promised myself that some day I would write a book about London.

The trouble was that so many had thought of it before. My colleague Mr. George Kamm has delved into a hundred books about London during his able searchings (which I acknowledge with most sincere gratitude) for the historical references in this volume. A bibliography of available works on London would include some fifteen hundred, with authors ranging all the way from Geoffrey of Monmouth and William FitzStephen to E. V. Lucas and Thomas Burke, by way of Defoe and a multitude more, without counting all the novelists and essayists, diarists, biographers and historians whose descriptions of London life were incidental to their wider purposes. Fielding and Dickens, Addison and Lamb, Pepys and Evelyn, Boswell and Macaulay—the grand parade of London's translators would stretch (if allowance were made for the wide spacing that artistic egos demand) from Temple Bar to Savoy Hill, where Wells, Bennett, Chesterton and Priestley would join the long line, a few yards behind Conan Doyle (' It is my belief, Watson, founded upon experience, that the lowest and vilest alleys of London do not present a more dreadful record of sin than does the smiling and beautiful countryside.' And it was on an alluring background of Sherlock Holmes's London that the case occurred with the fine side-issue that ' the husband was a teetotaller, there was no other woman, and the conduct complained of was that he had drifted into the habit of winding up every meal by taking out his false teeth and hurling them at his wife '). The procession of writers on London also has foreign contingents: Frenchmen from Taine to Paul Morand, Americans from Benjamin Franklin and Washington Irving to Christopher Morley and John Mason Brown.

The literature of London is short of nothing except in the category of the Grand Survey. During two thousand years of history, those by FitzStephen and Stow are the only works properly ranking as that. Besant's survey of nineteenth-century London was colourful but unbalanced and incomplete, because by then London had sprawled too widely for full tabulation by any one man. In the twentieth century it would need a whole department of a Ministry, or the staff of an Encyclopædia. In any case, the drafting of even a minor survey was beyond my time, talent and inclination. I embarked on an unambitious volume of impressions from the crowds and streets and characters of London in the nineteen-twenties; somewhat on the lines of Ned Ward's *The*

London Spy in the sixteen-nineties. A quarter of the book was written when somebody did exactly that, and did it better: Mr. James Bone's *London Perambulator* appeared. So the project for a book on London was put into limbo. Nothing remained from the idea except an occasional nagging that disappeared with the war and would never have returned if I had not seen an exhibition of pictures which the organisers, the Central Institute of Art and Design, had called ' The Londoner's England.'

To fulfil that title entirely, an exhibition would need thousands of subjects instead of hundreds. But this exhibition had the gist of it, in that the pencils and water-colour brushes of many artists revealed, not just the showplaces at the core of London, but a blend from the buildings and byways in most metropolitan districts, and beyond them, in the Home Counties which Londoners from, say, Hampstead, know better than they know, say, Greenwich. There were squares, markets, churches, bridges, palaces, parks, theatres, pubs, inns, vistas, roofscapes, streets, alleys, river-fronts and sea-fronts, quadrants and crescents, houses and rows of houses from several hundred years of architectural history; all (or nearly all) depicted with finer understanding than the camera could attain. It was a contribution to the topographical art of London, wider in its radius than the *Microcosm* of Pugin and Rowlandson, issued by Ackermann in 1808, and the equally famous *London As It Is* of Shotter Boys, issued in 1842. As such, it deserved to stay on collected record. It became for me an excuse for reviving, from the limbo of lost intentions, the project of a book on London; but with the labour halved, since half the number of pages would be filled by artists. It did not work out that way: the time given to finding and selecting, for the general pattern I wanted, further pictures from sources other than the exhibition; to getting the final collection adequately reproduced amid the heart-breaking state of the printers' (especially the colour-lithographers') programmes during 1946 and 1947; to visiting every one of the originals of the pictures; and (even with help from Mr. Kamm and others) to finding the facts behind the artists' façades—all that has taken more time than would have gone into a hundred thousand words of consecutive text.

This happened in despite of good offices from the Central Institute of Art and Design, which had organised the Londoners' Exhibition and been financed by four brewing corporations in commissioning hundreds of works of art for it. I mention the names of these brewing corporations—Messrs. Barclay, Perkins, Messrs. Courage, Messrs. Watney, Combe, Reid and Messrs. Whitbread—with real gratitude and a clear conscience. As owners of the copyright in many pictures, they gave me, with friendly wishes, whatever was required in publication rights: that and no more. There is not, and never has been, a bargain for any subsidy for the book, direct or indirect. Because they are public-spirited, I presume that Messrs. Whitbread, Messrs. Watney, Combe, Reid, Messrs. Courage and Messrs. Barclay, Perkins brew good beers. It would be

9

untrue to say that all beers taste alike to me; but I could not distinguish by taste one brand of beer from the others that are served in London. If there are public-houses among the Plates in the book, it is only because pubs are a cherished part of London life, and because these particular pubs were well-drawn and typical of their districts, or had a history. If there are likewise one or two breweries, it is because these breweries were notable (and readily available) details in the composition. It was a joy to discover, for instance, that one of the best Londoners of them all, Dr. Johnson, ' bustling about with . . . a pen in his buttonhole,' had helped to sell a brewery for Mrs. Thrale, and in so doing had invented the phrase ' wealth beyond the dreams of avarice.' Moreover, beer is in London life an ingredient as inevitable as it is companionable: witness Hogarth's outlook in his print of Beer Street—that beer invigorated and led to jollity, whereas misery and madness attended upon the Gin Lane which in his day dispensed, for next to nothing, the crude, raw Hollands that had come to London with Dutch King William.

The Londoner's England exhibition was well-planned and had a fine assembly of subjects and artists, but it was not enough for my purpose of assembling a pattern that would include only buildings as they now are, after the war and the blitzes. All the Plates in the book conform to that purpose except the Guildhall façade which is used (in Mr. Sydney Jones's sketch) to decorate the half-title page for the first section (here, a bomb destroyed the top tower, soon to be restored, without which the cropped Guildhall would seem unhappy as a symbol of City government during five hundred years). The Guildhall, like the Tower, St. Paul's and the Abbey, was among the few famous, oft-drawn show-places which, because of history or magnificence, had to go into the composition. It did not seem essential to include, among the widespread contents, close-ups of various nineteenth-century edifices that are renowned for their function rather than their architecture: Barry's Houses of Parliament, for instance, and the neo-Gothic Law Courts. The omissions of well-known buildings which I regret are the Inns of Court and Stationers' Hall (as a liveryman of the Worshipful Company of Stationers, I should have liked a water-colour of this). But these were badly bombed, and it seems that before very long they will be restored to something like what they were; in which case any sketch of the dilapidations would not be contemporary. What I wanted was a mixture of lesser buildings and scenes that had not been drawn often but could strike remembered chords from Londoners. ' Sir,' said Dr. Johnson (who held that to be tired of London was to be tired of life), ' if you wish to have a notion of the magnitude of this City, you must not be satisfied with its great streets and squares but must survey its innumerable little lanes and courts. It is . . . in the multiplicity of human habitations that the wonderful immensity of London consists.'

To be comprehensive was impossible; the more so because, in the past fifty years, the motor-car and motor-coach, together with increase of population and the growth of dormitory towns, have multiplied by four the province of South-East England which is familiar to Londoners. Brighton, Southend and the High Streets of some country towns are as much part of the Londoner's England as Trafalgar Square. Faced with all that, no editor of a picture-book could do more than collect, on the basis of what was attractive and available, subjects that appealed to himself and combined charm with a degree of topographical balance. On looking over the early proofs I was appalled by the omissions. At one stage I would have abandoned it all if the publishers had not spent so much on making plates in the different processes best suited to individual pictures. The same reason prevented abandonment later, when I heard that, by another publishing coincidence, a volume of London topography covering much of the same ground was in preparation by the Oxford University Press. By then, some of the Plates and Notes for *The Londoner's England* were already printed. That other work, the first volume of *Recording Britain*, appeared in the autumn of 1946, as part of a series which was designed to emphasise the pleasant, pre-war England which was passing. In that sense it contrasts with my assembly of pictures of buildings that have survived the war. Also, it had a wider scope in monochrome but contained a good deal less of colour-lithography. On the other hand, the illustrated lay-out for *Recording Britain*, and the presentation of its Notes by Mr. Arnold Palmer, were rather similar to mine. After reading just two of Mr. Palmer's Notes, I have carefully read no more, in case they should give me imitative ideas. I noticed, though, that the reviewers praised Mr. Palmer's text for its urbanity. So I have been at pains to ensure that mine shall not be urbane.

Meanwhile, the preparation of *The Londoner's England* has been an attractive diversion, if only for the talks with people learned in local history, and the tracking down of odd incidents in the lives of eminent Londoners of literature; whether it was Pepys kissing on the mouth the crumbling skeleton of a long-dead queen, or Dr. Johnson (yet again) being singularly unsuccessful as an amateur pyrotechnist and disturber of the peace. I am more than conscious that it is the artists who are the main begetters of the book. Even so, the sequence as edited may be too little architectural for those who like their Wren, Vanbrugh and Nash undiluted, and on the other hand what Joe Gargery called ' drawd too architectooralooral ' for those to whom London represents the tide of human existence, to-day and yesterday.

Metropolitan architecture, however, projects from human history. The Halls of the ancient Livery Companies, for instance—Stationers, Fishmongers, Goldsmiths and the others—are excellent assets to the City, but in function they are no more than repositories of phantom tradition. Their liverymen elect the City Council, which to-day has a purely local influence; and when food is ample they dine hugely on occasion, because liverymen in the Middle Ages dined hugely. By custom they are City Freemen; as ratepayers, they belong to Kensington, Reigate, Bishop's Stortford or wherever else. Their status comes from a tradition which (as happens more often in London than in any other capital city) has outlasted the reality by hundreds of years. They are as much an anachronism as the top-hats and black tail-coats of the boys at Eton, perpetually in mourning for King George the Third. They and their buildings are all that survive from the potent City Guilds which were able to send Kings and Chancellors packing; maintain free corps that rallied to the cry of ' Prentices and Clubs '; fight internal wars for the causes of Free Trade and Protection; and become, in commercial combination, an Estate of the Realm backing whatever ruler gave them the business charters they demanded. They adopted the young Richard II as ' The Londoners' King ' after Lord Mayor Walworth, in the royal presence, had killed Wat Tyler in Smithfield; but when Richard in later life upset their economics, they let him be displaced by Henry Bolingbroke. Hence, partly at the City's instigation, the Wars of the Roses, during which the Guilds lent money to both sides in turn. Because he paid the royal debts to merchants, they supported for a brief while Richard III, notwithstanding their outcry against the murder of the Princes in the Tower. Even when the chartered Merchant Adventurers were supplanting them, they could still do much to foment another Civil War by their rioting against King Charles's ministers, and by financing Parliament's armies, while incidentally giving to Cromwell's men the nickname of Roundheads, borrowed from the close-cropped hair of their militant apprentices. From all this, there remain only the ornamental Livery Companies, their opulent Halls and the endearing larder-names of some City thoroughfares that once were fastnesses of the provision trades: Bread Street, Milk Street, Poultry, Fish Street Hill, Mincing Lane.

The book is a patchwork made up from detail selected among the layers of nineteen hundred years of architectural history: Norman, Gothic, Mediæval, Tudor, Elizabethan, Stuart, Palladian, Georgian, Regency, Victorian, Edwardian, Functional, Metro-Goldwyn. Much of the detail might serve for one of those film cartoons that demonstrate growth and statistical incidence through animated diagram. An animated cartoon of London could open with a Roman wall emerging from Celtic mist. Inside the wall, well-ordered erections of stone and wood rise above the marshes: they are dented by Boadicea's fury but expand into the Londinium of the reference by Tacitus: ' greatly celebrated for the number of its merchants and the abundance of its supplies.' Darkness falls over the settlement when the Romans withdraw (query: did it, as in the theory of Sir Lawrence Gomme, stay compact with the Roman wall for two hundred years, buying safety with vigilance and the trading facilities which the Saxon invaders needed? Or was it over-run and left desolate until the Saxons adopted urban life?). The settlement, still within the Wall, reappears in the era of Alfred, and is bridged to a smaller pattern across the river—Southwark. Saxon, Danish and Viking armies thrust at both settlements (hence ' London Bridge is Falling Down '). A third settlement appears up-river: the Westminster of the Saxon kings, which Norman and Plantagenet kings develop. New styles of edifice, Norman and Gothic, spread from it to within the merchants' Wall.

The process of building persists in face of riots, recurring fires and the existence of manor-farms inside a City parcelled between the Barons, the Guilds and the Church. The pace of internal expansion accelerates with the abolition of the City's monasteries and Church manors. It continues through the alarum of the Armada and the further alarum of Civil War (when London cheers a Lord Protector's victory and a King's execution, only a few years before it hoots the Protector's son and cheers a King's restoration). Outer expansion leaps over the Wall and the river, and proceeds far beyond. The diagram of London City spills through Charing Cross to take in Westminster; it absorbs Southwark, moves down-river beyond a Greenwich that changes from royal pleasaunce to a port and shipyard. The City's inner core is rotted by plague and the worst of the Fires: almost at once (as time runs) it rises in greater magnificence. The speed of outer development quickens—Westminster and Holborn acquire ordered squares and quadrants, disordered stews and purlieus. The diagram races outward to absorb the green and brown of villages and noble manors: Chelsea, Kensington, Hammersmith, Chiswick in the west; Marylebone, Hackney, Islington, Hampstead, Highgate in the north; Clapham, Camberwell, Croydon in the south; everywhere between Whitechapel and Ilford to the east. The rush to build redoubles under the impetus of steam and steel: the London which, late in the nineteenth century, shouts itself hoarse at the Jubilee of an old, stout, primly dignified little queen, is a greater welter of palaces, churches, mansions, slums, factories, wharves and warehouses than the world has ever known.

Thus, Little Arthur's Animated Cartoon of London's growth; not including the holes made in the diagram by destruction from the air, and not showing how, as townlets and villages are absorbed, their rôle as rural refreshment for London is transferred to places deeper in the coloured counties. London and the Home Counties now comprise one-seventh of the area of England; they have nearly one-half of England's population.

Into what London will Little Arthur, child of to-day, grow up? The planners have imagined and ably drafted for him a yet bigger and better-ordered London, belted across the middle with green fields and artificial brooks. If such a London arrives and is settled without benefit from prosperity and a rise in the national birth-rate, it may become to England what Athens is to Greece and Vienna to Austria: too big a head for too small a body.

But will that yet greater London arrive? There is a pause in the headlong race to build, at a moment when building and restoration are needed as never since the Great Fire.   With that, there can be diagnosed among Londoners an odd fatalism, an unaccustomed readiness to accept, without protest in the lusty spirit of ' Prentices and Clubs,' a new despotism deriving from small tyrannies and inquisitions.   The people of London, in what is claimed as the century of the common man, have mislaid some of the colour and vigour of London life. London in the late nineteen-forties seems *diminuendo*, not quite herself.   If the recovery delays too long, the faint foreshadowing of Macaulay's New Zealander, contemplating the ruins from London Bridge, may reach the English Channel; a shadow that is poignantly evoked in Mr. Ralph Hodgson's poem, ' Time, You Old Gipsy Man ':

> Last week in Babylon,
> Last night in Rome,
> Morning and in the crush
> Under Paul's dome;
> Under Paul's dial
> You tighten your rein—
> Only a moment,
> And off once again. . . .

But Rome, many centuries after the departure of the centurions, has outlasted her empire and the shrinkage of her Faith: as the capital of a diminished race, she remains glorious.   Outside the hazards of the atomic age, the odds are that London, younger than Rome by a millennium, has more than that much longer for her moment in time.

LONDON : CENTRAL

THE GUILDHALL   *SYDNEY R. JONES*

NELSON'S COLUMN, which like St. Paul's dome, Big Ben and Eros in Piccadilly, has become a symbol of London to Londoners everywhere, was set up in 1843 amid a chorus of discord. It impressed the crowd that flocked to Trafalgar Square, but the *cognoscenti* loudly deplored the design by William Railton (an ecclesiastical architect steeped in the antiquities of Greece and Rome), who had imitated one of the Corinthian pillars of the Temple of Mars Ultor, erected in the Forum at Rome by Augustus after he took vengeance on the murderers of Julius Caesar. The French historian Taine, in his *Notes on England*, wrote of ' that hideous Nelson, stuck on his column with a coil of rope in the form of pigtail, like a rat impaled on the top of a pole.'

The Column itself is 154½ feet high; above it Nelson adds a further 16 feet. The statue is of stone, and the capitol is in bronze from cannon in the sunken *Royal George*, of which Cowper wrote in his poem beginning, ' Toll for the brave! ' The bas-reliefs at the base of the Column are of the Battle of the Nile, the Bombardment of Copenhagen, the Battle of St. Vincent and the Death of Nelson. The four Victorian lions at the corners were added by Landseer.

Nelson's Column, and Trafalgar Square in general, are taken as the focal point from which so-called Central London radiates eastward and northward, and the West End radiates westward and immediately southward. The artist painted his water-colour while looking north-eastward from Warwick Street through Cockspur Street.

The Two Chairmen Tavern, on the right, was built in 1683 : it used to preserve an historic signboard dating from Charles II's reign, showing a sedan-chair carried by two chairmen, with the royal monogram on the door. At the western end of Warwick Street was Warwick House, home of the widow of Charles Talbot, only Duke of Shrewsbury, whose father had died of a wound received in a duel with George Villiers, the notorious second Duke of Buckingham (Talbot's mother, dressed as a page, is said to have held the horse of her lover Villiers). It was in Warwick House, near enough to Carlton House for supervision, that the Prince Regent installed his difficult daughter, Princess Charlotte. She escaped from it in July of 1814, after she had broken off her forced engagement to the Prince of Orange. The eighteen-year-old Princess rushed alone across Cockspur Street and jumped into a hackney coach, which took her to the house of her mother (Caroline) in Connaught Place. Her father was furious, her mother tearful; London at large was amused at the incident and sympathetic to the ladies.

The Plate opposite is from a water-colour by S. Dennant Moss.

THE THEATRE ROYAL, DRURY LANE, has for centuries been among the most famous theatres in the western world. The present theatre, as a structure, is the fourth to be built on the site. Benjamin Wyatt designed it in 1810 ; but the long Ionic colonnade was added later.

The first Drury Lane theatre was built for Thomas Killigrew and his company under Charles II, and opened with Beaumont and Fletcher's *The Humorous Lieutenant.* Nell Gwyn appeared in this play later, and Pepys records that he kissed her in the theatre. It was totally burnt down in 1672. Drury Lane's greatest period came with the second theatre, designed by Wren ; on its sturdy arches the present theatre still stands in spite of the bombs that hit it in 1940. In the reigns of Queen Anne and the first three Georges, the theatre and its rival, Covent Garden, were favoured under Court licence ; and visits to the Theatre Royal formed part of the programme for kings and heirs apparent, as for rank and tattling fashion. Attempts on the lives of George II when he was Prince of Wales, and on George III, were made inside it. David Garrick became a partner in 1747 and delighted the public for nearly thirty years ; others who played here in the most notable period of English acting were the 'incomparable' Mrs. Siddons, Kynaston, Betterton, Colley Cibber, Kemble, Bannister, Macklin, Mrs. Brace-girdle, Peg Woffington, Kitty Clive, the Duke of Clarence's Mrs. Jordan and the Prince of Wales's Perdita Robinson, as well as Grimaldi the clown.

Sheridan was manager from 1776 and soon became chief proprietor ; he rebuilt the theatre in magnificent style to Holland's design, and the third Drury Lane was opened in 1794. While at the House of Commons in 1809 he heard that the theatre was burning ; and the oft-told tale is that, having hurried there and found it impossible to save the building, he sipped wine in a coffee-house opposite. A friend praised his coolness ; and he asked, 'May a man not be allowed to drink a glass of wine at his own fireside?'

Edmund Kean's first appearance in the present theatre was as Shylock in 1814 : the cast was poor, there had been only one rehearsal, the atmosphere was hostile, the house less than a third full ; but the curtain came down to terrific applause for the upstart Kean. Macready, Webster, Mme. Vestris, Sims Reeves, Henry Irving and Ellen Terry were among later stars. Augustus Harris ('Druriolanus') as manager made the Lane the central home of Christmas pantomime, with Dan Leno, Herbert Campbell, Little Tich and Marie Lloyd in his casts. The more modern history of Drury Lane includes Arthur Collins, who set the town gaping with flamboyant melodramas and vast scenic sets (race-tracks, swimming pools, real railway-trains and the rest) ; in the 1930's, Mr. Noel Coward's cavalcading and Mr. Ivor Novello's luscious, large-scale musical comedies featuring the good young man who nearly died but set his teeth and seldom cried ; and, from 1939 to 1946, the hive-headquarters of Mr. Basil Dean's Ensa.

The Plate opposite is from a water-colour by E. B. Musman.

ST. PAUL'S, COVENT GARDEN, deserves a long essay, preferably by Sir Osbert Sitwell. Inigo Jones designed it for the fourth Earl of Bedford, who disliked spending money and was said to have asked for a plain edifice ' not much better than a barn.' ' You shall have the handsomest barn in England,' replied Jones, and proceeded to plan a Tuscan-style building to form the west side of a piazza that had the garden of Bedford House for southern border. The church was at first much admired, but Horace Walpole (to whom Mr. Speaker Onslow told this anecdote) could ' see no beauty ' in it and particularly criticised the portico facing the Market square, which, intended by Inigo Jones as the main entrance, is in fact ' a sham ' because the ecclesiastical authorities insisted on the altar occupying the customary position at the east end and consequently the true entrance is on the west side, as seen in Mr. Pimlott's picture. Fire destroyed the church in 1795, but it was faithfully rebuilt to the original design by Thomas Hardwick, father of the architect who was to plan Euston Station.

Bishop Juxon, who attended Charles I on the scaffold, consecrated the church. Charles I's statue (now at the top of Whitehall) was hidden in the vaults during the Commonwealth by a brazier called Rivett, who had been told to break it up. An early rector was Simon Patrick, who tended the sick and buried thousands of dead during the Great Plague. Hustings for Westminster elections in the eighteenth century faced the church : Charles James Fox spoke from them often.

In no other London church, except the greater St. Paul's and Westminster Abbey, were so many famous people buried : Lely, John Kneller, Girtin, among painters, Wycherley the dramatist, Dr. Arne the musician, Samuel (*Hudibras*) Butler, Grinling Gibbons the sculptor, Sir Robert Strange the engraver, and a host of noted actors, including Charles Macklin and Squire Bancroft. The ashes of Ellen Terry are also there. Among the great and the good was buried in 1742 a magdalen of whom *The Gentleman's Magazine* recorded that she had ' helped the gay gentlemen of this country to squander upward of £50,000.'

St. Paul's the lesser has for long been known as ' the actors' church.' Scenes from Bernard Shaw's *Pygmalion* were filmed in its portico. To-day's priest-in-charge, the Rev. Vincent Howson, acted with Sir Frank Benson and is secretary of the Old Bensonians. He fosters a growing, non-residential congregation : porters from Covent Garden, together with office-workers and players *en route* for matinées, attend his lunch-hour service on Wednesdays.

ST. PAUL'S, COVENT GARDEN   JOHN PIMLOTT

COVENT GARDEN MARKET is on the site of the ancient Convent Garden that belonged to the Westminster monks until the dissolution of the monasteries by Henry VIII. The seven acres of the garden were then granted to John Russell, first Earl of Bedford, who built his town house in the Strand, near to-day's Southampton Street. Under Charles I the fourth Earl laid out the site as a square, bordered on the north and east by a piazza which Inigo Jones designed. Sellers of fruit and vegetables set up a market in the square, and the Earl built sheds for them in 1632. For a century the market remained an affair of sheds and stalls on which herbs, snails and parrots were sold, as well as garden produce from the nearby villages. The nucleus of the present buildings was erected by the sixth Duke of Bedford in 1830. The ninth Duke added the English flower-market on the Tavistock Street side; the French flower-market appeared in 1903.

Despite the then ramshackle market in the square, the Piazza of Covent Garden was a fashionable address during the late seventeenth and early eighteenth centuries: the Earl of Orford, Bishop Berkeley, Sir Kenelm Digby, the Duke of Richmond and the painters Lely and Kneller lived there. Richard Steele, in *The Spectator* of 1712, describes a visit by people of quality to a puppet-show in the square. Later, the district became better known for its roystering. Edward Gibbon, referring to his four 'costly and dangerous frolicks' from Oxford to London, says that when at fifteen he visited the City as a gentleman-commoner at Magdalen, 'I was too young and bashful to enjoy, like a manly Oxonian in town, the taverns and bagnios of Covent Garden.' The district was famous for its supper-rooms in the nineteenth century; and local night-life persisted until the 1930's.

The Market itself opens at midnight for the reception of produce. Its peak hours are around 8 A.M., when the approaches are choked with growers' lorries unloading, retailers' vans and costers' barrows filling up, and flower-women hurrying off to their pitches with arms full of flowers. Porters nonchalantly balance high towers of laden fruit-baskets on their heads (at championship meetings the winners carry upward of twenty baskets). They quench their early-morning thirst in the local public-houses, which are open for Market workers only, from 5 A.M. to 9 A.M. In warehouse cellars near-by, women shell peas and broad beans for the big hotels.

COVENT GARDEN MARKET

FRANCES MACDONALD

ST. MARTIN'S-IN-THE-FIELDS and the Rev. Dick Sheppard, its vicar from 1914 to 1927, evoked this comment in a biography by R. Ellis Roberts: ' He made the church the most widely known in London, he himself the best-known and most widely loved parson in England ; hundreds of thousands of men, for whom religion had meant routine, boredom, mumbo-jumbo, something desiccated and dead, found it was exciting, moving, helpful, alive. St. Martin's became the church of the soldiers and down-and-outs ; the church of the classes and the masses ; the church of fellowship and privacy . . it became the refuge for the unhappy and the home of the homeless.' Dick Sheppard kept the crypt open all night for the down-and-out (by day he lent part of it as a Button Boys' Club for messengers and hotel-pages), had a bookstall in the porch, broadcast sermons from the church, produced an annual Mystery Play in the chancel, and founded the *St. Martin's Review*, to which many eminent writers contributed.

The original parish of St. Martin's-in-the-Fields was separated from St. Margaret's, Westminster, by Henry VIII, to save himself from the distress of the funerals that passed his palace in Whitehall on the way to St. Margaret's. James Gibbs, who rebuilt an older church in the early eighteenth century, treated the building externally as a temple ; but his steeple, rising from the roof instead of the ground, is often criticised. Nevertheless his design influenced church architecture for a century, especially in America : St. Martin's was the model for St. Paul's Church on Broadway, New York.

George I was a churchwarden in the period when one side of the church looked down on the royal mews (later cleared to make Trafalgar Square). The steeple is surmounted by a crown to signify the royal parish. Those buried in and around St. Martin's-in-the-Fields include Nell Gwyn (in a nameless grave beneath the chancel), Thomas Chippendale, Nicholas Hilliard the first English miniaturist, George Farquhar the dramatist, Roubiliac the sculptor, and Van Somer the portrait-painter. Francis Bacon was christened in the old church, and so was Sir Winston Churchill, father of the great Duke of Marlborough.

"St Martins in the Fields"

ST. MARTIN'S-IN-THE-FIELDS   *FRANCES MACDONALD*

Plate 7

INTERIOR OF ST. PAUL'S CATHEDRAL

The artist worked from a cradle that had been slung under the roof to mend a large hole caused by the bomb which, in October 1940, fell into the Choir, damaging the Sanctuary with masses of fallen masonry.

LORD METHUEN

THE INTERIOR OF ST. PAUL'S was completed in 1697, only twenty-two years after the foundations were laid. In the distance is the West Door above the church-yard and Ludgate Hill. A hundred feet above the floor in the middle distance is a section of the Whispering Gallery, which has for visitors the phenomenon that if they talk close to the wall their words are clearly heard all round the great circumference of the gallery.

The whole interior was decorated in the late nineteenth century with sumptuously coloured mosaics that detract from the wood-carving by Grinling Gibbons and the lovely iron-work by Tijou. Nevertheless Christopher Wren, as architect, intended the cupola to be lined with mosaic.

A congregation of five thousand can worship in the cathedral : a thousand of them under the glorious dome. Many of the special services at St. Paul's belong to national or ecclesiastical history : the rejoicing in 1789 for the supposed recovery of George III from madness ; the taking of the oath of allegiance by thousands of scarlet-coated Volunteers in 1803, when Napoleon's invasion was expected hourly ; the royal service on November 11 in 1918 for the Armistice ending the ' Great ' War ; the funerals of Nelson and Wellington, whose massive tombs lie in the crypt with those of Reynolds, Turner, Lawrence and other famous artists ; in 1710, Dr. Sacheverell's sermon against the Dissenters, for which he was impeached ; in recent times, the interruption by a Canon (who dramatically left the cathedral with a thousand supporters) of a sermon by the ' modernist ' Bishop Barnes. There was occasional criticism of the conduct of services in former days—thus, Charles Kingsley wrote in 1847 : ' The place breathed imbecility and sleepy life in death, while the nineteenth century went roaring on its way outside.' At that time there was a charge for admission.

St. Paul's is famous for its Deans : among them John Donne (whose monument in Old St. Paul's was the only one left intact by the Great Fire of London), Henry Hart Milman, Robert Gregory and, in contemporary times, W. R. Inge. The Canons have included Sydney Smith and Dick Sheppard. Handel played the organ to mark the innovation of pedals in 1720 ; Sir John Goss and Sir John Stainer were among the organists in the nineteenth century. As for Sir Christopher Wren, his tomb in the crypt was properly inscribed by his son : *Si monumentum requiris, circumspice.*

THE MONUMENT, commemorating the Great Fire of London and erected to Christopher Wren's design in 1671–1677, is 202 feet high, the reputed distance from the baker's shop in Pudding Lane where the Fire started : the distance and other facts are recorded in Latin on panels of the pedestal. The inscription on the north side was given in 1681 an added line attributing the Fire to Papists : James II had it effaced, it was restored under William and Mary and finally removed under William IV. On the west side of the pedestal is a bas-relief by C. G. Cibber (father of Colley Cibber the actor-dramatist) showing Charles II succouring the City of London. The drawing opposite looks from Eastcheap down Fish Street Hill toward the Church of St. Magnus the Martyr. Pepys mentions the earlier church on the same site in a note on his visit to the Lieutenant of the Tower, ' who tells me that it [the Great Fire] began this morning in the King's baker's house in Pudding-lane, and that it hath burned down St. Magnes Church and most part of Fish-street already.'

Wren's drawings for the Roman Doric column of the Monument, preserved at All Souls', Oxford, show that he first intended the column to be left hollow, as a tube for an astronomical telescope fitted with a vast object-glass that had been given to the Royal Society ; but the height of 202 feet was insufficient for this purpose. A staircase of black marble leads up the interior to a balcony below the summit, from which there is a superb view over London. A cage was added to the balcony in 1842, after several people had committed suicide by throwing themselves from the top.

The square in which the Monument stands was formerly known as Monument Yard, at a corner of which was the chemist's shop where Oliver Goldsmith obtained employment in 1756 when he came to London, destitute after his period of vagabondage on the Continent.

THE MONUMENT, FROM EASTCHEAP   *KENNETH STEEL*

STAPLE INN, HIGH HOLBORN

TOM WAGHORN

STAPLE INN is described by Dickens in *The Mystery of Edwin Drood*, where Mr. Grewgious has offices in the inner quadrangle : ' Behind the most ancient part of Holborn . . . is a little nook composed of two irregular quadrangles, called Staple Inn. It is one of those nooks the turning into which out of the clashing street imparts to the relieved pedestrian the sensation of having put cotton in his ears, and velvet soles on his boots. It is one of those nooks where a few smoky sparrows twitter in smoky trees, as though they called to one another, " Let us play at country," and where a few feet of garden-mould and a few yards of gravel enable them to do that refreshing violence to their tiny undertakings.'

The Inn dates from medieval times, having been built as a hostelry of the wool ' staple,' where wool was weighed and excise dues collected. The façade, believed to be the oldest half-timbered one in London, was added in the sixteenth century at about the period when the building passed into the hands of the Ancients of Gray's Inn. The back was encased in brick during the Regency ; the front, after various tinkerings, was restored to the original design in 1886, after the Inn had been bought by that omnivorous London landlord, the Prudential Assurance Company. The main buildings were again reconstructed in 1937, though the old front remains. The inner quadrangle was destroyed during the recent war by a bomb, but the east and west wings of the front quadrangle survive. Trees and a circular ornamental pond decorate the cobbled square. An old notice-board, preserved under the archway from High Holborn, reads : ' The porter has orders to prevent old clothes men and others from calling articles for sale. Also rude children playing &c. No horses allowed within this Inn.'

Dr. Johnson lodged for a short while in Staple Inn, having moved from Gough Square, Fleet Street, on March 23, 1759, when he wrote to Miss Porter : ' I have this day moved my things and you are now to direct me at Staple Inn, London. . . . I am going to publish a little story book which I will send you when it is out.' This was *Rasselas*, written in the evenings of one week to meet the expenses of his mother's illness and funeral.

ST. GILES'S-IN-THE-FIELDS, the third church on the site, succeeded its neo-Gothic predecessor in 1733, when Henry Flitcroft totally rebuilt the church for a Duke of Bedford. Flitcroft, known as ' Burlington Harry,' was a character of the period who started life as the son of William III's gardener at Hampton Court, trained as a joiner and attracted the attention of the Earl of Burlington by falling from a scaffold in the latter's house ; whereupon the Earl compensated him with employment as a draughtsman on an edition of Inigo Jones's designs which was published at the Earl's expense. Flitcroft's name is perpetuated in that of an adjoining street.

The parish of St. Giles was originally called St. Giles-of-the-Lepers, from the hospital founded by Matilda, Henry I's Queen, which stood on the site of the church. When the hospital was demolished under Henry VIII, the name was changed to St. Giles-in-the-Fields ; and it stayed mainly in the fields for 150 years, although it was in this parish that the Great Plague broke out. Later came ' St. Giles's Rookery,' a warren of squalid slums, through which New Oxford Street was driven in 1846-1847. Some 2,850 people lived on one and a half acres of the Rookery ; shelter could be had at 3*d.* a night, and often fifty people slept in one room. Water had to be drawn from a large tank in one of the streets. Many of Hogarth's pictures of misery and vice were drawn from this neighbourhood. The sanitary authorities took action in the 1840's ; and a model lodging-house was erected by the Society for Improving the Conditions of the Labouring Classes.

The churchyard was closed in 1854, following a petition to the Home Secretary against its danger to the public health. In it are buried George Chapman, the Elizabethan friend of Ben Jonson, who inspired Keats's ' On First Looking into Chapman's Homer,' and the dramatic poet James Shirley (' The Glories of our Blood and State '), who with his wife had been driven by the Great Fire of London from his house in Whitefriars. Two months later the Shirleys both died in the parish of St. Giles, ' being in a manner overcome with affrightment, disconsolations and other miseries occasion'd by that fire and their losses.' Andrew Marvell, that bright star in the constellation of Caroline poets, lies buried under one of the pews in the southern part of the church. Two of Shelley's children by his second wife Mary Godwin (both of them doomed to die soon in Italy) were christened here in the company of Allegra, daughter of Byron and Claire Clairmont.

ST. GILES'S-IN-THE-FIELDS   *CHARLES GINNER*

LUDGATE CIRCUS, at the junction of Fleet Street, Farringdon Street, Ludgate Hill and New Bridge Street, gets its name from the King Lud of Celtic myth who might have built a gate in the wall round his settlement. Occupation of the area goes back into the historical mists: excavations by Sir Christopher Wren revealed a large Saxon cemetery, beneath which were Celtic remains above a lower layer of Roman remains and pavements. There was also on the site a bridge across the River Fleet, now an underground stream; and Ludgate Hill behind it formed a forty-foot cliff. The postern of Norman times was probably built before the Conquest; and in medieval times it was the link between London proper and the extension that began to sprawl towards Westminster. King John's turbulent barons rebuilt it in 1215, after they had entered the City and (according to Stow) pillaged the Jews. During four hundred years, until the gate was taken down in 1761, the chambers above it were a prison for City debtors. Lud Gate was rebuilt in Elizabeth's reign, and statues of the Queen and of the legendary King Lud were placed upon it; the statue of Elizabeth now adorns a doorway to the church of St. Dunstan-in-the-West, Fleet Street.

St. Martin's, on the right, was built in 1684 as one of Wren's City churches in his Plan for London after the Great Fire. Had that Plan not been vitiated by cheeseparing from the State and opposition from the property-owners, Ludgate Hill would have obtained the aesthetic advantage of a clear view of St. Paul's at the top. As Bowyer's Row, Ludgate Hill was a fashionable shopping centre in the seventeenth century. A style of walking affected by young City people became known in the mid-eighteenth century as the Ludgate Hill hobble. The long-famous hostelry of La Belle Sauvage, dating from the fifteenth century, was on its northern side.

The Circus itself was a late-comer in 1864-1875, when most of the old houses were pulled down. The disfiguring railway bridge overhead, on the line between Blackfriars and Holborn Viaduct, was built despite a petition to the City Corporation, bearing a thousand signatures. The King Lud Tavern on the left was originally owned and run by a Lord Mayor of London, Sir John Bell. It introduced to London's public-houses, some fifty years ago, the trade in 'quick lunches and snacks.' Obelisks in the Circus commemorate two Lord Mayors, both vigorous politicians of the late eighteenth century; John Wilkes, the demagogue, and Robert Waithman, a reformer whose linen-draper's shop stood at the corner of Fleet Street and New Bridge Street. A plaque marks the pitch where Edgar Wallace sold newspapers as a boy.

The Plate opposite is from a water-colour by Ruskin Spear.

SAMUEL WHITBREAD'S HOUSE formed (and still forms) part of the great brewery which was established in 1742 and was moved some years later from Old Street to the present site in Chiswell Street. It is recorded in a newspaper of the time that one Saturday morning in 1787 George III, accompanied by Queen Charlotte and three of the Princesses, visited Mr. Whitbread's brewery and spent two hours there. They were particularly interested in the steam-engine designed by Watt, in the stone cistern large enough to hold 4,000 barrels of beer, and in the horses. ' The walk ended in the house. Their Majesties were led to a cold collation as magnificent as affluence and arrangement could make it.'

Samuel Whitbread the first, founder of a dynasty, came to town from Bedfordshire. He entered the brewery as an apprentice, became its owner, rapidly extended the fame of its porter and stout (ale was not brewed here before 1834) and managed his business without a partner for fifty-four years. He was as noted in philanthropy as in brewing, and founded in Middlesex Hospital one of the earliest wards for the treatment of cancer. He was succeeded by his son Samuel, who distinguished himself as a social reformer in and out of Parliament: he was a follower of Charles James Fox, a strong advocate of Negro emancipation, of national education and of the extension of religious and civil rights. As chairman of Drury Lane's Theatre Committee after the previous playhouse was burned down in 1809, he tried out the innovation of attracting wider audiences by playing on every night of the year.

The house (middle left in the picture) is now part of the brewery's general offices. The premises have spread to the north side of Chiswell Street, and a tunnel under the road connects the vast cellars. Whitbread's have the right to supply the horses for drawing the Speaker's coach at a Coronation—a privilege dating from 1839, when Charles Shaw-Lefevre (later Viscount Eversley), a partner in the firm, was elected Speaker of the House of Commons.

Chiswell Street was described in 1838 as ' a very important thoroughfare of respectable shops' and as ' celebrated for the extensive foundry established by Mr. Caslon for the manufacture of printing type.' This foundry, opened in 1735, was the third to be established by the well-known type-designer William Caslon. His daughter married an original partner in Whitbread's brewery.

The Plate opposite is from a water-colour by Patrick Hall.

LONDON: WEST END

SHEPHERD MARKET, only two hundred yards from Piccadilly (up White Horse Street), is a fragment of old London with something about it of the atmosphere of a small market-town. It has a warren of old streets containing little shops that sell most things, the only insistently metropolitan parts of the market being a few dining-cum-night clubs.

The market was built about 1735 by an architect named Edward Shepherd, who placed butchers' shops in the lower parts of his main buildings and devoted the upper parts to song and dance. Shepherd intended his venture to form part of the notorious May Fair, which later gave its tarnished name to the larger, glittering district north and west of it. The May Fair, however, was finally closed before Edward Shepherd could finish his market; and the locality lost its clamour from stalls, sideshows, bagnios, prize-fighting, bull-fighting, bear-fighting, a ducking-pond and much else. Ned Ward in *The London Spy* had recorded of May Fair: ' In all the multitudes that I ever beheld, I never in my life saw such a number of lazy rascals, and so hateful a throng of beggarly, sluttish strumpets, who were a scandal to the Creation.' Excited orators in Hyde Park have since said almost as much about the later district of Mayfair.

The odd little market has been used as background for more than a few contemporary novels, including the late Sir Hugh Walpole's *The Joyful Delaneys.* Its name, in fact, went round the world during the late 1920's because of its association with *The Green Hat*: with that transient best-seller in mind, American tourists came to see the haunts of the brave, kind nymphomane who suffered for purity. A later association with America came during the recent war, when U.S. soldiers, largely from the Washington Club in nearby Curzon Street, thronged the several taverns in Shepherd Market. Of these latter, the best-known are Shepherd's Bar, where the telephone booth is an old sedan-chair, and Ye Grapes (shown in the foreground of the picture), where the saloon contains a glass frame full of coins that have been stuck on with beer: when the frame is full, the money is collected for charity.

Plate 13 opposite is from a water-colour by Charles Ginner.

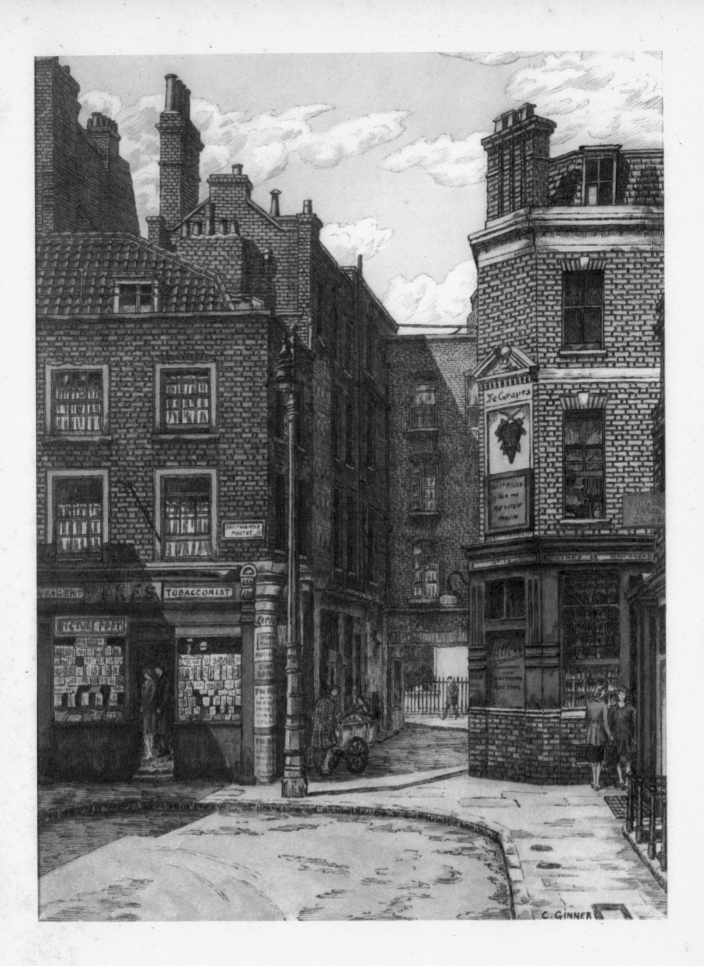

William A. Wildman

Berkeley Square was during two centuries a synonym for the life aristocratic. As the popular song had it :

> A house in Berkeley Square will suit us to the ground,
> We'll dine in state off silver plate with flunkeys standing round—
> With great, big flunkeys standing round.

Under the direction of John Evelyn, the square was built on the gardens of Berkeley House (replaced later by Devonshire House) in about 1698 ; but for long afterward the nightingale sang in Berkeley Square and the half-rural region around it. The water-colour shows, at the corner of Charles Street, part of the west side, which retains some of its eighteenth-century houses, excellently proportioned. Fixed to some of the iron railings are the link-extinguishers, shaped like trumpets, which were used by the link-boys who waited outside the mansions to light the path of diners-out. Among the plane-trees once stood an outsized statue of George III in the character of Marcus Aurelius. Thackeray's Marquis of Steyne had a house in the Square which was depicted in the *Yellowplush Papers* as 'Buckley Square.'

The corner house in the picture, No. 52, was the residence of Field-Marshal Lord Strathnairn, better known as Hugh Henry Rose, hero of the Crimean War and the Indian Mutiny. No. 50, next but one, was in the late nineteenth century the scene of the 'Berkeley Square Mystery' : a maidservant and a young gentleman were said to have died in it from fright, on seeing ghosts.

Lord Clive of India killed himself in No. 45. Other early residents were Horace Walpole, Charles James Fox and Lord Brougham. Fox figured in a fantastic procession which, with the Dukes of Bedford and Devonshire each in a coach-and-six, attended by trumpeters on horseback, paraded the square before returning to Devonshire House. Lord Clermont's house was a rendez-vous for the Prince of Wales (later George IV) and Mrs. Fitzherbert. Byron records how, after giving away the daughter of his attorney John Hanson to the half-mad Earl of Portsmouth, he returned with her to her father's house in Berkeley Square and ' drank a bumper of wine (wholesome sherris) to their felicity, and all that.'

Elsewhere, Berkeley Square is rapidly changing its face ; the eastern and southern sides are allotted to blocks of modern flats, car-salesmen, estate-agents, the shops of couturiers *et al*.

Charles Street, which runs into the Square on the left, is named after the seventeenth-century Earl of Falmouth, whose brother was the first Lord Berkeley of Stratton. Notable occupants have included Beau Brummell, Lord Lytton (who furnished a drawing-room to counterfeit a Roman chamber at Pompeii) and the Duke of Clarence before he became William IV. Anthony Trollope in 1864 was elected to the Cosmopolitan, a political and literary club that met twice a week in Charles Street and supplied to its members and their friends ' tea and brandy and water without charge.'

The Plate opposite is from a water-colour by William A. Wildman.

PICCADILLY CIRCUS: 'The Centre of the World' was for many years the grandiose claim that glowed in electric lights on the northern pavement, outside the London Pavilion. Paul Morand, a Frenchman who knew the pre-war West End better than most Londoners, called the Circus 'the navel of London.' Visitors from abroad and overseas tend to start their explorations from this centre of six great thoroughfares. Much traffic, crowds, cafés, restaurants and oyster bars, theatres, shops, flower-sellers, garish electric-signs and England's loveliest statue are blended into its personality.

It began as the first Regent Circus (the second was the present Oxford Circus), which took shape as part of John Nash's plan for a street of noble architecture reaching from Portland Place to the Prince Regent's home in the old Carlton House. Nash was obliged to let various builders modify his plan for most of Regent Street, but he made himself responsible for the Quadrant, that excellent curve whereby he swung Regent Street proper round to meet the line of what to-day is called Lower Regent Street. He placed on each side of the Quadrant an imposing colonnade; but in the result the shops beneath were in permanent gloom, and predatory characters loitered on the enclosed pavements. The Quadrant's 270 columns were therefore removed in 1848; and during the 1920's Nash's harmonious buildings were demolished by the town-planners in favour of a new Regent Street of massive stone and concrete, which was supposed to symbolise the twentieth century but which in current architectural taste is already outmoded.

Eros, the inspired small statue by Sir Alfred Gilbert, in the middle of the picture, is held in affection by all Londoners: its purpose as crown to the memorial for the philanthropic Earl of Shaftesbury, of mid-Victorian times, has been long forgotten. The Circus held informal celebration when Eros returned in 1931, after eight years' absence in Embankment Gardens to permit construction of Piccadilly's great new Underground Station. It underwent more exile in Surrey during the war years, followed by a further period when officials left it lying on a mattress in a dark room of County Hall. It was restored to the Circus in 1947.

Behind Eros is Swan and Edgar's, originally a tiny shop owned by John Swan in the early nineteenth century; here it hides the Piccadilly Hotel, built on the site of the old St. James's Hall, famous for its 'Monday Pops' and Christy Minstrels, where Wagner once conducted and where in 1870 Dickens gave his last Reading. The vista extends down Piccadilly to St. James's, and up Regent Street to the Café Royal (at the extremity of the right-hand curve), which was associated with the higher Bohemianism all the way from Whistler and Wilde to John and Epstein.

PICCADILLY CIRCUS   CLAUDE MUNCASTER

THE GOAT, STAFFORD STREET, is an old tavern (probably dating from 1686) on the site of the former Clarendon House, home of Charles II's harried Lord Chancellor. Of that 'best contrived, the most useful, graceful and magnificent house in England,' the diarist John Evelyn noted : 'The Chancellor gone, and dying in Exile, the Earl his successor sold that which cost £50,000 building, to the young Duke of Albemarle for £25,000 to pay debts. . . . This stately palace is decreed to ruin, to support the prodigious waste the Duke of Albemarle had made of his estate, since the old man died. He sold it to the highest bidder, and it fell to certain rich bankers and mechanics . . . I was astonished at this demolition, nor less at the little army of labourers and artificers levelling the ground, laying foundations, and contriving great buildings at an expense of £200,000, if they perfect their design.' The buyer was Sir Thomas Bond, whose building operations covered Bond Street, Albemarle Street, Grafton Street and Stafford Street ; 'he built a street of tenements to his undoing,' commented Evelyn on Bond Street.

One Matthew Tomlinson, in a will dated 1735, bequeathed 'the freehold tavern known as The Goat and the rent therefrom' to provide an annual sum for clothing 4 poor men and 3 poor women of the parish of St. George's, together with 3 poor men and 3 poor women of the parish of St. Martin's-in-the-Fields ; such persons to be clothed on the day of the month on which the testator died. Tomlinson's charity is still in the hands of trustees, and in 1945 15 men and 39 women benefited.

Before the war of 1914-1918 the smoking-room on the first floor became a favourite rendezvous for naval officers. Admiral of the Fleet Lord Fisher, as First Lord of the Admiralty in 1914, sometimes attended in mufti and talked to junior officers, many of whom did not recognise him. On the outbreak of war security demanded that the gatherings be moved to more private quarters ; as a result, the Goat Club was formed, with premises in New Bond Street.

THE GOAT TAVERN, STAFFORD STREET, OFF BOND STREET   *PHYLLIS DIMOND*

R UPERT STREET'S market, more paintable than the larger street-market in Berwick Street near-by, was sketched by the artist from the corner of Tisbury Court, looking toward Shaftesbury Avenue and the Globe and Apollo Theatres. The barrows in this casual street-market are mainly for flowers and vegetables ; but on a fine day in spring or summer many other wares are on noisy offer, from puppies to shoe-laces by way of glass and china, second-hand books, stockings and collar-studs. The frequenters come largely from the international population of Soho, though there is a sprinkling from the fluid crowd that waits for engagement outside the office in Archer Street of the London Orchestral Association. Rupert Street itself first appeared in the Rate Books of 1677, but there is no recorded origin for the market.

The name Rupert Street derives from Prince Rupert, Civil War cavalry-general who was the son of Charles I's sister, Queen Elizabeth of Bohemia. When Robert Louis Stevenson's Prince Florizel of Bohemia was ' hurled from the throne in consequence of his continued absence and edifying neglect of public business,' the author honourably retired him, after the adventures of *The Suicide Club* and *The Rajah's Diamond*, to a cigar-store in Rupert Street, much frequented by other foreign refugees. But this was probably in the better dressed (though still raffish) section of Rupert Street between Shaftesbury Avenue and Coventry Street, near or next to the chemist's well-known shop which in real life, from the 1890's until the 1930's, was open all night and famous for its pick-me-ups.

THE MARKET, RUPERT STREET, SOHO

E. B. MUSMAN

Plate 18

HYDE PARK CORNER, all but rural until the eighteenth century, is now the busiest traffic-point in the Empire. The low Ionic screen that forms the entrance to Hyde Park was designed by Decimus Burton and erected in 1828 over a road that forked northward to Tyburn and westward to Rotten Row (probably a corruption of *Route du Roi*). There was a toll-gate across the present Knightsbridge at what was formerly London's boundary, close to St. George's Hospital on the extreme left.

The oldest of the buildings is immediately right of the screen : Apsley House, long known as 'No. 1 London.' Lord Chancellor Apsley built it after buying the ground from the owner of an apple-store, an old soldier to whom George II had given the site for bravery at the Battle of Dettingen. The nation presented the house in 1820 to the Duke of Wellington, who installed iron shutters after the mob broke his windows during the 1832 agitation over the Reform Bill. The present Duke has given it to the Nation. Next, to the right, is 148 Piccadilly, a former residence of the Rothschilds ; in the gap farther to the right was No. 145, where the present King and Queen lived as Duke and Duchess of York—the house was later destroyed by a German bomb. Left in the distant foreground is the Royal Artillery

HENRY RUSHBURY, R.A.

memorial of 1914–1918, by C. S. Jagger; and on the right is Burton's triumphal Arch.

Hyde Park became fashionable for drives, rides and promenades under Charles II. In the Regency and under George IV the Corner and Rotten Row were rendezvous for Corinthians on horseback or in light cabriolets, and for sportsmen of the Tom and Jerry type described by the elder Pierce Egan. Under Queen Victoria the scene stayed fashionable but shed the sporting aspect. Sunday Parade in the Park was a social institution for broughams and other modish equipages, for the riders of well-groomed horses and for those who sauntered and decoratively idled. It so continued through the eras of the crinoline, the bustle, the picture-hat, the frock-coat and the morning-coat above the inevitable spats, and onward through the reign of Edward VII and that of George V until the late 1920's. The Park Parade was often the subject of music-hall song, including ' Captain Ginger ' :

When strolling in the Park, or riding in the Row,
I have to merely be polite to ladies whom I know.
' Ah, Countess, how-de-do ? '—
I knew her when a girl—

She sang in comic oprah long before she met the Earl.
There's the Duchess—*Dem !*—I almost made a fluke.
We nevah speak as we pass by—
It might upset the Dook.

ALBANY (it is not done to use 'The') reaches from a pleasant courtyard off Piccadilly to Burlington Gardens. It was for a century the most renowned of non-monastic strongholds for bachelors. Its main house, facing the Piccadilly side, was built *c.* 1763 for the first Lord Melbourne by Sir William Chambers, a notable architect who built the Pagoda in Kew Gardens and helped to found the Royal Academy. Henry Holland designed the long, double line of some sixty sets of chambers (shown in the picture) which in 1804 arose in the garden of what was then York House, and which were intended for single gentlemen.

Byron, with his manservant Fletcher, was an early inhabitant during his years of high fame and notorious entanglement. In his sitting room, records Mr. Peter Quennell in his admirable biography, were the silver urns he brought from Greece, his screen pasted with 'scraps' of actresses and boxers, a long table piled with books, a macaw and a crucifix. Here he read solidly, 'fortified by biscuits and draughts of soda-water,' between his drinking-parties and vast feasts. Here he was pursued by Lady Caroline Lamb : 'She comes,' wrote Byron, 'at all times, at any time, and the moment the door is opened, in she walks. I can't throw her out of the window.' Lady Caroline stated later that after burning Byron in effigy, she had visited his rooms at Albany disguised as a carman, and that he had embraced her and whispered passionate endearments. Macaulay (who thought nothing of taking a country walk to Greenwich and its whitebait suppers) and Bulwer Lytton lived there, and continued the literary flavour which has never quite left Albany. Later residents in the nineteenth century were Gladstone and Squire Bancroft. Albany tenants from fiction have been many. Dickens, in *Our Mutual Friend*, gave Fledgeby rooms on the second floor.

Ladies, married or unmarried, did not become acceptable as residents until years after 1914–1918 ; and fervent argument by masculinists among the seven trustees (elected to serve as freeholders by the thirty or more proprietors of groups of chambers) attended the change. Dames of the British Empire, women-novelists, and other ladies have since joined the tenantry. Most of the sets of chambers consist only of a sitting-room, two bedrooms, entrance hall and bathroom ; and the married often occupy separate sets of rooms on opposite sides of a landing.

G. L. FROST

TRAFALGAR SQUARE, FROM THE SOUTH-WEST

FRANCES MACDONALD

TRAFALGAR SQUARE, so orderly in its lay-out, began in disorder. From 1829 onward, the clearing of the former conglomeration of royal mews, haphazard housing, shabby purlieus and Mr. Cross's Zoo lasted twenty years. The plans for the square were part of the scheme by John Nash to connect Whitehall with the area around the British Museum; but the idea lapsed until Charing Cross Road was built in 1887 on a more westerly line. The square was, however, linked with the lower end of Nash's new Regent Street by the construction of Pall Mall East.

The National Gallery, centred in the picture's distance, was built in 1832-1838; Nash entered a competition for it, but William Wilkins obtained the award. The purpose of the Gallery was to house Sir Julius Angerstein's collection of 38 paintings, bought in 1824 for £57,000, at the suggestion of George IV, to form the nucleus of a National Collection. Since then the National Gallery, without much money from the State but with the help of bequests from millionaires and others, has acquired more than 4,000 works of fine art. Ably directed in most periods, it has become one of the institutions of England. On the grass strip outside it stands a statue (in replica) of George Washington, presented to London by the State of Virginia in 1921.

The Royal College of Physicians, erected on the west side to Sir Robert Smirke's design, paid the Crown an annual rent of a peppercorn for many years after it was built in 1825. On the east side the church of St. Martin's-in-the-Fields is next to the modern but well-proportioned South Africa House, behind Nelson's Column. The idea of a column was probably suggested by William IV, who loved the Navy and cherished Nelson's renown. Sir Edwin Landseer's rather meek lions were placed at the four corners of the pedestal in 1866. Lesser statues in the square are of Sir Henry Havelock, Sir Charles Napier, General Gordon and, at the north-east corner, the equestrian statue of George IV, originally intended for the top of the Marble Arch, that stood until 1850 in front of Buckingham Palace. On a platform of granite below the northern wall of the square are the official 'Secondary Standards of Length' set up in 1875 under the direction of the Astronomer Royal.

For sixty years Trafalgar Square has been the centre for mass-meetings, orderly or disorderly. The most famous was held by London's workless on Bloody Sunday, November 13, 1887, when heads were broken by police batons, the cavalry were called out but did not charge, John Burns (then known as 'the man with the red flag') and Cunninghame Graham were among the arrested speakers, and the young, red-bearded George Bernard Shaw was among those prominent. Since then speakers of all varieties, from Suffragettes in 1906 to the advocates of a Second Front in 1942-1943, have harangued their followers from the plinth of Nelson's Column.

CLEVELAND ROW, at the bottom of St. James's Street, is a prolongation
westward of Pall Mall after passing St. James's Palace.   Farther westward
it overlooks the Green Park, which until the middle of the seventeenth century
was part of the private grounds of the Palace.   Only one building then stood
between the Palace and Piccadilly—Berkshire House, given by Charles II
to his mistress of the moment, Lady Castlemaine, later Duchess of Cleveland ;
hence the name Cleveland Row.   The Green Park was opened to the public by
Charles II ; and on its St. James's side smaller houses arose, some for the less
opulent aristocracy and some that became modish lodging-houses (the lodgers
included various gentlemen friends of Harriette Wilson, author of the deplor-
able but entertaining *Memoirs*).

Most of the houses date from the early eighteenth century, and were
renovated under the Regency.   Up the lane and next to the building in the
foreground of the picture is Garrett House, with curious projecting windows
imitative of the latticed windows in the Orient that enabled occupants of a
harem to look down the street.   In the dining-room of a neighbouring house
occurred the quarrel between Sir Robert Walpole as Prime Minister and Lord
Townshend as Secretary of State, which Gay is supposed to have satirised
in the quarrel-scene between Peachum and Lockit in *The Beggar's Opera*.
Among several notable householders in Cleveland Row was Admiral Lord
Rodney, who destroyed the French invasion craft at Havre in 1759 and was
victorious in other sea-fights against the French and Spanish fleets.

CLEVELAND ROW, ST. JAMES'S

TOM WAGHORN

CONSTITUTION HILL has no proved origin as a name : it first appears
on a map of the early eighteenth century.   Its high ground had been
a site for artillery when, in 1554, Queen Mary's troops opposed Sir Thomas
Wyatt's rebels, who had advanced on the City through Kensington. The
eminence was also used by Parliament men in the Civil War as part of the
fortifications round London.   Three attempts on the life of Queen Victoria
were made on Constitution Hill : in 1840 by an eccentric named Oxford, who
was detained as a madman; in 1842 by John Francis, who was ordered to
be hanged, beheaded and quartered (the four quarters to be disposed of as Her
Majesty should deem fit), but who by virtue of royal clemency was instead
transported to Tasmania for life ; and, also in 1842, by a certain Bean, who
got only eighteen months' imprisonment.   Sir Robert Peel, thrown from his
horse in Constitution Hill after calling at Buckingham Palace, died on the
next day (1850).

The so-called ' Pimlico Arch ' in the foreground formed part of Decimus
Burton's design (1828) for a noble road crossing from Hyde Park to the Green
Park ; and originally it stood directly opposite the stone screen in front
of Hyde Park. It was modelled on the Roman Arch of Titus. Burton
intended a quadriga for the top of the arch, but amid protest a fearsome
equestrian statue of the Duke of Wellington was placed there. ' *Nous sommes
vengés*,' said a French officer who inspected the statue. It was removed to
Aldershot in 1883, when the decision was taken to move the Arch itself across
the open space to its present position ; and in 1912 the Quadriga designed
by Adrian Jones was erected on the summit.

The gates of the arch are supposed to be opened for royalty only, but the
military funeral of one of the gate-keepers (who are always chosen from
ex-Service men) was once permitted to pass through them. A police-station
in the southern sector of the arch accommodates the constables on local
traffic duty ; the gate-keeper lives inside the northern sector.

The Plate opposite is from a water-colour by Henry Rushbury, R.A.

WEYMOUTH MEWS is curiously enclosed between the backs of mansions in Portland Place and Harley Street. On the Portland Place side is the former residence of Field-Marshal Earl Roberts, while on the Harley Street side are the houses occupied for varying periods by J. M. W. Turner and the eminent Victorian statesman Sir Stafford Northcote, afterward first Earl of Iddesleigh. The mews, which links Weymouth Street with New Cavendish Street, still has some stables that are used as such for hacking in Regent's Park. A long lease of the land on which the Dover Castle tavern stands was granted in 1778 by the third Duke of Portland to Robert and James Adam, architects, and Abraham Dakin, plumber, for a rental of ten shillings a year, paid quarterly. This must have been one of the many building plots taken over by the Adam brothers for the construction of Portland Place and the adjoining area. Portland Place, to the south was originally closed by Foley House, whose site the Langham Hotel now occupies; Lord Foley had obtained in his lease of the ground from the Duke of Portland an undertaking that no buildings should be erected to interrupt the view northward to Hampstead and Highgate, and Portland Place was therefore given the exact width of Foley House's frontage. The Cavendish–Harley estate surrounding Cavendish Square, a little to the south, had already been developed by Edward Harley, second Earl of Oxford (son of Queen Anne's Minister), and other prominent Tories, who wanted to exploit the district of Marylebone Fields, stretching northward from the present Wigmore Street.

The neighbourhood, in fact, was semi-rural until late in the eighteenth century, and Marylebone Gardens were a rival to Vauxhall Gardens. Dr. Johnson once visited Marylebone Gardens with a friend who wanted to see the fireworks; but the evening turned out to be showery, and the pyrotechnic display was cancelled. Dr. Johnson was very annoyed. ' This,' Boswell records him as saying to his companion, ' is a mere excuse to save their crackers for a more profitable company. Let us both hold up our sticks, and threaten to break those coloured lamps that surround the Orchestra, and we shall soon have our wishes gratified.' Some young men who heard him thereupon tried violence and lit some fireworks, ' to little purpose.' Thus, Boswell records, did Dr. Johnson appear as the ringleader of a disturbance, though not as an effective pyrotechnist.

The Plate opposite is from a water-colour by S. Dennant Moss.

LONDON: NORTHWARD AND WESTWARD

WELL WALK, HAMPSTEAD: the name, like that of Flask Walk nearby, derives from the medicinal waters which, discovered by a local doctor late in the seventeenth century, were put into flasks and sold all over London. These waters raised the status of Hampstead, which in Henry VIII's time was a village said to be inhabited largely by washerwomen who laundered the clothes of the City gentry. A memorial in Well Walk records that a chalybeate well here was given in 1698 by the Hon. Susanna Noel and her son Baptist, third Earl of Gainsborough (then an infant), ' to the use and benefit of the poor of Hampstead.' Exploitation followed when the trustees of the gift granted a concession to one John Duffield. Well Walk was laid out with its fine row of lime-trees, and a set of Assembly Rooms with Pump-room, band, dancing, gaming-tables and bowling-green attracted fame and fashion to Hampstead, which was honoured by visits from the Kit-cat Club.

The Spa lost repute for a while when ' low character ' brought petty crime to it; and the Great Room in Well Walk became a place of worship. Later, the Wells were revived and a new set of public rooms arose farther west, including the houses seen in the picture, which formed the ballroom. Johnson, Samuel Richardson, Garrick, Fielding and Goldsmith were frequenters of Hampstead Spa during this second flowering.

Well Walk in the early nineteenth century had many lodging-houses; and it was with a kindly postman called Benjamin Bentley that John Keats and his two brothers took rooms in 1817. The house was on part of the site now occupied by the Wells Hotel, the railings of which are prominent in the picture. Only a few minutes' walk downhill was Wentworth Place, the house of Keats's friends Charles Brown and Charles Dilke (editor of the *Athenæum* and, later, manager of the *Daily News*). Keats made his home with Dilke and Brown after his brother Tom died; and when, early in 1820, he had his first hæmorrhage, he was given a sofa bed near a window from which he could see the passers-by. In a letter to his sister Fanny he writes: ' I mus'n't forget the two old maiden Ladies in Well Walk who have a Lap dog between them that they are very anxious about. It is a corpulent Little Beast whom it is necessary to coax along with an ivory-tipp'd cane.'

John Constable lived at No. 40 Well Walk from 1827. 'A comfortable little house,' he called it, with a view from the drawing-room, extending from Westminster to Gravesend, which he considered to be unsurpassed in Europe.

Plate 24 opposite is from a water-colour by Rupert Shephard.

PADDINGTON GREEN, much larger than it now is, remained a village green until early in the nineteenth century, when the opening of the Grand Junction Canal brought holiday-makers and, later, settlers. It was celebrated in the old ballad, ' Pretty Polly Perkins of Paddington Green.' During the Commonwealth the villagers erected a rampart between the pond and the Harrow Road, so as to command that entrance into the capital.

Greville House was the most prominent of the few houses round the Green in the eighteenth century ; it is now No. 22, directly behind the greenkeeper's hut toward the right of the picture. Emma Lyon, Nelson's future Lady Hamilton, lived in it for some years under the protection of Charles Greville, nephew of Sir William Hamilton, whom she met at Greville House.

Ignatius Paul Pollaky, a famous detective from Austria in the pre-Sherlock Holmes period, lived on the east side of the Green at No. 13 (now 12A) ; he is celebrated in *Patience*, where W. S. Gilbert refers to ' the keen penetration of Paddington Pollaky.'

St. Mary's Church, left in the picture, was built between 1788 and 1791, and is the third parish church of Paddington. It is composed of yellow brick with a Doric front, and has a small cupola. The first contractor was found to be a bankrupt and all four of his walls cracked, but it was finished at a cost of £6,000. Its predecessor, on a site about eighty yards to the north-west, had been a church of St. James, built by Sir Joseph Sheldon and Daniel Sheldon ; it was in this church that William Hogarth made his runaway match on March 23, 1729, with Jane, the daughter of his art-master Sir James Thornhill.

For many years, until about 1838, St. Mary's maintained the curious custom of throwing bread and cheese from the church to spectators on the Sunday before Christmas. The charity was begun by two spinsters who purchased five acres of land to this use in memory of a time when they had been in great need. In the old graveyard behind the church lies the great actress Sarah Siddons, whose funeral in 1831 was attended by some five thousand people ; a statue of her by Chavaillaud, after the painting by Reynolds, was unveiled on the Green by Sir Henry Irving in 1897. Close by her grave her faithful dresser ' Patty ' was buried. Among others who lie here are Benjamin Haydon, the diarist and painter of immense religious pictures, who on his release from the debtors' prison lodged on Paddington Green before his suicide in 1846 ; Joseph Nollekens, the parsimonious sculptor whose busts were the rage in the 1770's ; Nollekens' father, the painter ; and William Collins, painter of the Tate Gallery's *As Happy as a King* and father of the novelist Wilkie Collins.

Near the Green, off the Harrow Road, was the foundry in which the much-ridiculed statue of the Duke of Wellington, costing £30,000, was cast ; it was drawn in 1846 by twenty-nine horses to Hyde Park Corner, where it was hoisted to the top of Decimus Burton's Arch.

The Plate opposite is from a water-colour by Charles Ginner.

CAMPDEN HILL SQUARE: AN IMPRESSION.   This pleasant square of Georgian houses climbs abruptly from Holland Park Avenue toward what G. K. Chesterton, in *The Napoleon of Notting Hill*, called ' the great grey Water Tower that strikes the stars on Campden Hill.' The square was begun in 1827, twenty years before the Water Tower, and was first called Hanson Square after the builder of the original nine houses.   The name was changed to Notting Hill Square and, in 1893, to Campden Hill Square in response to a petition from the inhabitants.   Though the name Campden Hill was not recorded for the district until 1827, it perpetuates an old association through Sir Baptist Hicks, first Viscount Campden and a benefactor of the poor of Kensington, who bought (or, it is sometimes said, won by wager) Campden House from Sir Walter Cope in about 1612.   Campden House abutted on what is now Church Street ; it and the more famous Holland House near-by were for many years the only two buildings of consequence in this part of Kensington.   The whole area was countrified until William and Mary converted Nottingham House into Kensington Palace.   At about the same time several local springs were discovered.   The present Aubrey House adjacent to Campden Hill Square, much altered and remodelled, is the Wells House which was built in 1698 to exploit the waters containing Epsom or Glauber salts ; and the square is on ground that belonged to Wells House.

The houses on the southern, hilly side of the square had a good view of the racecourse called the Hippodrome, which opened on the other side of Holland Park Avenue in the month when Queen Victoria was crowned.   The natives of the Kensington Gravel Pits village (now Notting Hill Gate) insisted on their right of way across the course, and broke down the enclosure with hatchets. The Hippodrome closed in 1841 and the area became covered with houses.

The rural garden has always been a feature of Campden Hill Square : a comic drawing by Henry Alken, Junior, of a tailor being chased for shooting birds on Sunday (called *The Hunted Tailor*, 1834), shows a man climbing over the palings. The character of the residents seems never to have changed from an early description of ' professional and business men, retired soldiers, clergymen and ladies living alone.' They have always been steadfast in maintaining the Square's amenities and their own privileges as controllers, through a committee, of the garden. In the 1860's they took action against some scholastic establishments in the square, and banned ' Hoops, Cricket, Football, Quoits, Trap and Ball, Archery, Catapults, Throwing Stones, Hide and Seek, Throwing Ball and Flying Kites.' They did not permit dogs in the communal garden until 1895, and then only if they were ' under proper control.' They declined in 1897 to allow illuminations to celebrate the Jubilee, but showed instead their patriotism by planting a copper-beech. In 1905 they protested against the use of Campden Hill as an unofficial trial-ground for the new-fangled motor-cars. They have placed on a tree in the south side of the garden a tablet stating that J. M. W. Turner executed many water-colour sketches there.

CAMPDEN HILL SQUARE : AN IMPRESSION

URSULA EARLE

THE SWAN INN, BAYSWATER ROAD, with its arresting façade and occasional tables in the open courtyard, wears a more zestful air than that of the average public-house. Whether by accident or brewers' design, its lease-holders have for long been specialists in welcome ; among them was the late Maisie Gay, buxom comédienne of the halls and of Mr. Cochran's revues.

The Swan, indeed, is the only surviving relic of the Flora Gardens (later known as Victoria Gardens), which flourished from about 1790 until the tall houses of Lancaster Gate were erected in the 1860's. They included the ' Physic Garden,' where ' Sir ' John Hill, the versatile eighteenth-century apothecary, botanist, writer and quack doctor, grew the plants for the herb medicines which he sold at great profit. Hill was, according to Walpole's *Letters*, ' made gardener of Kensington, a place worth £2,000 a year,' on George III's acces-sion. He had unsuccessfully tried acting and playwriting ; and when a farce of his was hissed off the stage he turned his fluent pen against Garrick, who replied in the epigram :

> For physic and farces, his equal there scarce is ;
> His farces are physic, his physic a farce is.

The Bayswater Road, constructed over the route of the Roman road from London to Exeter, was formerly bounded by turnpikes, on the west at Notting Hill Gate and on the east at Tyburn. This was a favourite stretch for Claude Duval, the highwayman whose supposed gallantry to the ladies he waylaid did not save him from being hanged in 1670 on Tyburn Tree, the site of which is marked by a brass inset in the roadway close to Marble Arch (the last execution here was in 1783). Along Bayswater Road from Marble Arch, in 1860, was laid one of the two first tramways in London, constructed as an experiment by an American called Train. It ran on step-rails raised fourteen inches above the ground-level, so that vehicles could cross only with great difficulty. Such an outcry arose from carriage-owners and carters that within a year Mr. Train was ordered to remove his new-fangled method of locomotion.

The Swan faces the part of Kensington Gardens (where foxes were hunted as late as 1798) containing an Italian garden with fountains, at the head of Long Water, as that section of the Serpentine is called. Sir James Barrie, before he moved to Adelphi, had a near-by house opposite Kensington Gardens, to which he owned a private key. The association is recalled by Sir George Frampton's statue of Peter Pan by the side of Long Water. Another local resident, in Lancaster Gate, was Bret Harte.

Two hundred yards east of the Swan is the Victoria Gate into a section of Hyde Park well known for displays of tulips in spring and dahlias in autumn, and for the Dogs' Cemetery, dating from 1880, when the Duke of Cambridge, as Ranger of the Park, obtained permission for his wife to bury a pet dog there. Other burials followed until the practice was stopped in 1915.

CHARLES GINNER

THE SWAN, BAYSWATER

EUSTON ARCH, A GATEWAY TO THE NORTH : The architecture and design of most of London's main railway-stations are regrettably undistinguished : the high Doric arch in front of Euston Station, with the Great Hall of the station itself, forms a pleasing exception. This arch, reminiscent of the gateway to the Acropolis at Athens, was designed by Philip Hardwick, architect to the Duke of Wellington. The impressive entrance was flanked on either side by two lodges, which were linked by ornamental gates (three of the four lodges still stand). The Arch, constructed of stone from Yorkshire, cost £35,000 ; and objection was made to ' the great expense of this ornamental entrance.' The word EUSTON was carved in gilt on the front, amid some outcry, in 1870, when a reconstruction of the station distorted the spacious conception of Hardwick. Behind the Arch, his son completed in 1849 the Great Hall, partly inspired by the interior of the Palazzo Vecchio in Florence. Its panelled ceiling is said to be the largest of its kind in the world. In it stands a large statue of George Stephenson, inventor of the railway engine, whose son Robert planned the original Euston Station.

The Bill to authorise the London-Birmingham Railway was rejected by the House of Lords in 1832 on the ground that it was undesirable to force the proposed line ' through the land and property of so great a proportion of dissentient landowners and proprietors ' ; but it was passed the following year, and the first section—from Euston to Boxmoor in Hertfordshire—was opened in 1837 with three trains a day. Until 1844, locomotives of incoming trains were taken off at Chalk Farm, and the coaches were then attached to an endless rope that lowered them down the incline to Euston, the speed being regulated by brakesmen. Euston to-day, headquarters of the London, Midland and Scottish Railway, covers twelve acres ; and an average of 60,000 passengers arrive and depart daily in 120 main-line trains.

Part of the ground beneath the station was known in the eighteenth century as Church Field ; among those buried in it were George Morland and John Hoppner the painters, and Lord George Gordon, that queer firebrand who led the violent anti-Catholic riots of 1780, became a practising Jew and ended a strange career in Newgate Prison. Euston Road dates from 1757 and has been associated with other enterprises in transport. It saw the trial run of Sir Goldsworthy Gurney's road-locomotive in 1825 ; Shillibeer's first London bus-service in 1829 from the Yorkshire Stingo tavern in Marylebone to the Bank ; and Hancock's first steam-bus in 1833.

EUSTON ARCH   *E. B. MUSMAN*

Plate 29

HENRY VII'S CHAPEL, WESTMINSTER ABBEY :
Charles Lamb, in one of the *Last Essays of Elia* (published in 1833), laments that ' in no part of our beloved Abbey can a person find entrance (out of service time) under the sum of two shillings.' The main sections of the Abbey are now open to all—the nave and transepts of the lofty building, begun about 1243 by Henry III, who pulled down the previous Norman Abbey to make room for a more splendid shrine to his patron Edward the Confessor ; the Sacrarium and Altar ; Poets' Corner in the South Transept, holding memorials or tombs of many famous writers between Edmund Spenser and Thomas Hardy ; and the grave of the Unknown Warrior, buried on Armistice Day in 1920. Fees are still demanded, however, to see the Royal Chapels, including the Coronation Chair on which the nation's monarchs since Edward the Confessor have been crowned.

Henry VII's Chapel was founded in 1503 by Abbot Islip on the King's behalf, to serve as a mausoleum for Henry himself and for Henry VI, whose body he intended to bring from Windsor. The Lady Chapel of the old Abbey was demolished for that purpose ; and the coffin of Henry V's Queen, Katherine of Valois, was disinterred and temporarily placed by her husband's tomb. For some unexplained reason, it found no final resting-place until 1878 : the inevitable Pepys records, rather ghoulishly, seeing the exposed corpse ' by particular favour, and I had the upper part of her body in my hands, and I did kiss her mouth, reflecting upon it that I did kiss a queene, and that this was my birth-day.' In the garden of the old Lady Chapel had stood the house in which Chaucer, as Henry IV's Clerk of the Works, lived for a few years before his death in 1400 (he is buried in the South Transept of the Abbey).

The fan-vaulting of the nave-roof has by some been called the finest example of the stonemason's craft in the world. The interior contains a superb grille by Torrigiano, round the tomb of Henry VII and his wife Elizabeth of York. In the side-aisles are the rather overpowering tombs of Queen Elizabeth and Mary Queen of Scots, together with a stone coffer for the bones of two children presumed to be Edward V and Richard of York, the princes murdered in the Tower.

The bay at the extreme east of the Chapel is dedicated to the R.A.F. pilots in the Battle of Britain : a roll of honour is kept in it, and the armorial badges of the 63 squadrons engaged are in a new stained-glass window. A small round hole in the wall, caused by a fragment of the bomb that fell in October 1940 in Old Palace Yard between the Chapel and the Houses of Parliament is framed in glass as a memento. This bomb also bent the sword in the hand of the bronze statue of Richard Cœur de Lion (seen in the picture), which was designed by Baron Carlo Marochetti, the refugee sculptor from Piedmont who was patronised by the Prince Consort. The Victorian Bishop Lightfoot condemned its existence and expressed surprise that in the shadow of Parliament there should be erected the statue of ' a man who cared nothing for laws or judicature or constitution . . . a ruffian in real life.'

The Abbey's octagonal Chapter House, completed in 1253, is on the left in the picture. Here the monks met regularly before the dissolution of the Abbey as such in 1540, when the Chapter House passed to the possession of the Crown. It was used as the meeting-place of the House of Commons until 1547, after which it became for three hundred years a depository for State Papers.

HENRY VII'S CHAPEL, WESTMINST

S. DENNANT MOSS

KNIGHTSBRIDGE GREEN : The small Green, at the Knightsbridge end of Brompton Road, is said to have been the site of a pit in which victims of the Plague were buried in 1665. Its triangular patch of gravel still has a few trees, though the railings were taken in the late war. The dignified building overlooking the Green is Tattersall's, the famous headquarters of horse-sales.

The founder of the firm, Richard Tattersall, was stud-groom to the second Duke of Kingston. In 1766 he set up his own business as an auctioneer of horses in premises behind St. George's Hospital, Hyde Park Corner ; and by his efficiency and probity he soon attracted an aristocratic clientele, including the leading members of the Jockey Club. He paid the then vast sum of £2,500 for the celebrated racehorse Highflyer, and on the foundation of its winnings and reputation he started a stud-farm which brought him much prosperity. He became a friend of George Prince of Wales, whose stud he sold, and an intimate of the set around Charles James Fox. Having acquired political ambitions with his wealth he bought *The Morning Post*, but lost heavily on that venture.

Under Richard Tattersall's great-grandson the firm moved in 1865 to its present premises, where until 1939 its auctions of polo-ponies and hunt-studs every Monday (and on Thursdays in the Spring) brought buyers from all over the world. Precisely 130 lots were offered on each occasion. Watched by fashionable crowds in the balcony of the great covered yard, the horses were paraded round the cupola which, crowned with a bust of George IV as a young man, stands over an ornamental pillar bearing a life-size bronze fox— a quaint memorial, long known as ' the palladium of Tattersall's.' On Sunday afternoons, particularly those immediately preceding the Derby and the Ascot races, Society thronged to view the horses which would be auctioned the following day. The yard has since been converted to other purposes, and Tattersall's retain only their offices in the building on the right ; blood-stock sales are confined to Newmarket. To the left of the portico is the old Subscription Room, formerly the centre from which all betting on the turf was regulated : two such rooms were originally opened by Richard Tattersall in Hyde Park for members of the Jockey Club.

Antique shops cluster in the neighbourhood of the Green. A stone's-throw eastward in Knightsbridge, north of Lowndes Square, is the site of Spring Garden, described by Defoe in *Moll Flanders*. Here too was The World's End, a famous drinking-house mentioned by Congreve in *Love for Love*. Pepys knew the tavern well ; his visit on May 9, 1699, was memorable because ' this day I first left off both my waistcoats by day and my waistcoat by night, it being very hot weather, so hot as to make me break out, here and there, in my hands, which vexes me to see, but is good for me.' The very last entry in his Diary, three weeks later, records : ' Thence to the World's End, a drinking-house by the Park ; and there merry, and so home late.'

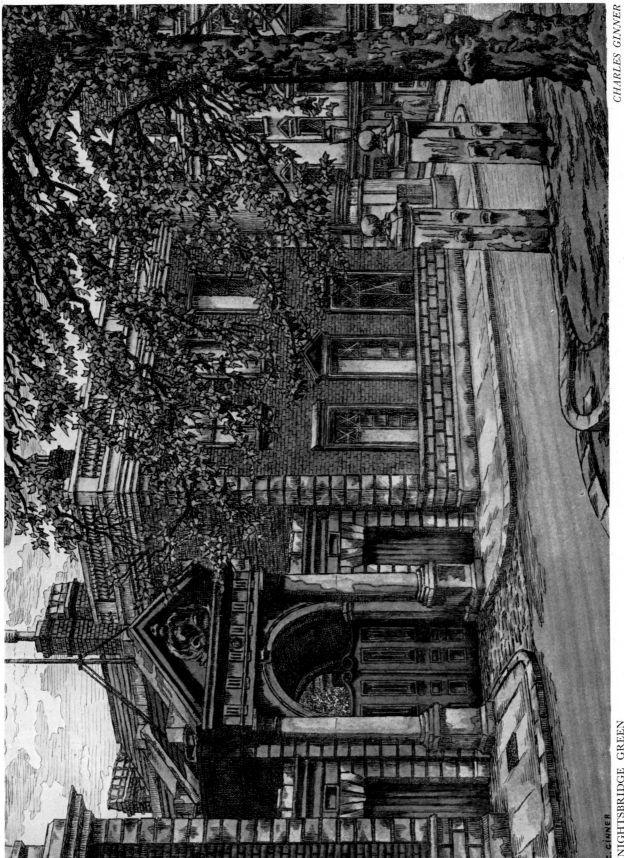

C. GINNER

CHARLES GINNER

KNIGHTSBRIDGE GREEN

PELHAM CRESCENT

CHARLES GINNER

PELHAM CRESCENT, which curves gracefully from the South Kensington section of the Fulham Road, is part of the estate owned by Smith's Charities, a trust originating in the seventeenth century when a rich salter named Henry Smith left £1,000 to purchase land ' for the relief and ransom of poor captives being slaves under Turkish pirates ' and a further £1,000 to be invested ' for the use and relief of the poorest of my kindred.' During the eighteenth century the site of the Crescent was occupied by nursery-gardens that looked southward to a terrace of pleasant little houses, called Amelia Place after the Princess Amelia.

Pelham Crescent itself was named after the family of the Earl of Chichester, one of the trustees. It was built in the 1820's by the architect George Basevi, Disraeli's first cousin, who had designed the houses in Belgrave Square ; his most important work was the Fitzwilliam Museum at Cambridge.

Edward John Trelawny, the friend of Shelley and Byron, whose flamboyant *Adventures of a Younger Son* became a classic, moved to No. 7 after the publication in 1858 of his *Recollections of the Last Days of Shelley and Byron*. He had saved Shelley's heart from the burning pyre on the shore near Via Reggio ; and after sailing to Greece with Byron he joined with gusto in the exploits of the Greek revolutionary chieftain Odysseus, and took charge of Byron's body at Missolonghi. Millais painted him as the old sea-captain in his picture *The North-West Passage*, which Trelawny heartily disliked, as it showed him as a bent old man huddled in a coat ; whereas, in fact, he remained to the end of his long life an upright giant who never wore an overcoat and walked five miles a day, from Brompton into Town and back.

Guizot the historian, Premier of France under Louis-Philippe and lover of the Princess Lieven, lived at No. 21 after his flight from Paris in the revolutionary year 1848. A group of nineteenth-century actors were inhabitants of the Crescent for varying periods ; among them were Charles Mathews the comedian, his wife Mme. Vestris, and Alfred Sydney Wigan, who, in 1836, played the original John Johnson in Dickens' *The Strange Gentleman* at the newly opened St. James's Theatre. The theatre to-day gives residential distinction to Pelham Crescent through Dame Lilian Braithwaite, Mr. Emlyn Williams and Mr. Oliver Messel.

CHEYNE ROW, CHELSEA: Away from the King's Road the riverside streets of Chelsea retain their old tranquillity. Cheyne Row (the name derives from a Lord of the Manor of Chelsea who died in 1698) has the atmosphere of a century ago. The terrace of ten houses on the left of the picture was built in 1708 upon the bowling-green of either the Feathers Inn or its neighbour the Three Tuns.

Richard Mead, the distinguished physician who attended Queen Anne, George I, Sir Isaac Newton and Sir Robert Walpole, and wrote treatises on hydrophobia and the plague, lived at No. 22, being followed there by the then Duke of Kent—'a good-natured man, but of very little consequence,' commented Jonathan Swift. The Row is most frequently associated with Thomas Carlyle, who took No. 24 (the first house before the portico on the left in the picture) in 1834, at a time when there were no houses opposite. 'The street is flag-pathed, sunk-storied, iron-railed, all old-fashioned and tightly done up,' he wrote to his wife. The rent was £35, and he constructed a sound-proof room where he could work undisturbed. During his forty-seven years in the house, the most notable literary people of the day visited him, including Tennyson (who liked to smoke clay pipes in the garden), Herbert Spencer the philosopher (who stopped coming after a few visits, as he disliked Carlyle's mannerisms), Dickens, Thackeray, and Leigh Hunt, who lived round the corner in Upper Cheyne Row with (to quote Carlyle) 'his sickly large wife and a whole school of well-conditioned wild children.' Here, too, came Emerson, Mazzini and Chopin, who played on the Carlyles' piano.

The line of trees in the Row were threatened with destruction in Carlyle's time : his wife was so incensed that she told a workman she would bring a pistol and shoot him if he started cutting them down. The present trees were similarly threatened in 1927, but all except two were saved. Boehm's statue of Carlyle can be seen in the distance in Chelsea Embankment Gardens. On the site of a Roman Catholic church, hidden by the house in the foreground on the left, was Orange House, where William de Morgan had a famous pottery before he turned novelist. A branch of Josiah Wedgwood's factory was established on a site between Cheyne Row and the King's Road late in the eighteenth century ; and here the thousand-piece dinner service ordered by the Empress Catherine II of Russia was decorated by Thomas Bentley, Wedgwood's partner, who had a house in Little (now Upper) Cheyne Row.

Cheyne Row was recommended in 1925 as 'especially worthy of preservation' by the Royal Commission on Historical Monuments, which saved it from demolition.

CHEYNE ROW, CHELSEA

CLIFFORD HALL

Clifford Hall.

TRYON STREET, CHELSEA, formerly Keppel Street, was renamed in 1913 after Vice-Admiral Sir George Tryon, who went down in the *Victoria* when he ordered the manœuvre which brought his flagship into collision with the *Camperdown* in 1893. The street is a turning off the King's Road to the north, immediately opposite the tree-lined Royal Avenue, planned by Wren to connect the Royal Hospital (which he had built for Charles II) with Kensington Palace.

The King's Road was originally Charles II's private road, by which he travelled expeditiously to Hampton Court Palace. Chelsea was then mainly rural, and the royal highway ran between fields and scattered farms. Energetic action by the Lord of the Manor, Sir Hans Sloane, brought in 1719 the grant of free access to it for local landholders and residents. Footpads and highwaymen abounded, and patrols were established to protect the public. A newspaper of 1749 criticised the normal patrol maintained by order of the Commissioners of the Chelsea College (the Royal Hospital) and summoned a meeting of the Gentlemen of Chelsea to petition for the posting of eight armed men ' in the Centry Boxes at proper Distances along the Road.' A farm-house on the site of the present terrace between Dovehouse Street and Carlyle Square was the scene of a notorious robbery and murder in 1771. About 1775 Sir John Fielding, the blind magistrate at Bow Street (half-brother of the novelist Henry Fielding), organised watchmen ; but the danger seems to have continued, for in 1778 a carpenter to the Board of Works was attacked and died from a pistol-shot. The road remained private until 1830.

The early nineteenth century saw many market-gardens and nurseries arise along the King's Road, which soon gained a dubious reputation in church quarters, for at its western end lay Cremorne Gardens, where much ale and sherry were drunk, there were alcoves for assignations, the dancing was held to be ' unbridled,' curious sideshows abounded ; and—greatest attraction of all— there were spectacular balloon-ascents. These latter were sometimes marred by fatal accidents ; as when, in 1873, a Belgian billed as ' the Flying Man ' fixed himself into a contraption consisting chiefly of a pair of huge wings and was hoisted into the air at the bottom of a rope hung from a balloon. The machine, on being cut loose over Sydney Street, crashed to the ground by St. Luke's Church, the foolhardy aeronaut being killed.

In the neo-Gothic church of St. Luke's, four hundred yards westward from Tryon Street, Charles Dickens was married to Catherine Hogarth.

The Plate opposite is from a water-colour by Joseph McCulloch.

Queen's Head
Tryon St
Chelsea

THE OLD WINDMILL, BRIXTON, has also been called Ashby's Mill, Brixton Mill and the Merry Brixton Flour Mills. This attractive relic, London's last tower-windmill, was built in 1816 and was worked until the newly-built houses round Blenheim Gardens took the wind out of the mill's sails in 1863. The building was then used for storage until 1901, when a gas engine was installed to work the mill. The custom was with local inhabitants: as late as 1900 there were old people living nearby who in youth had brought their gleanings from the wheatfields for crushing at Ashby's Mill. The grandson of the original Ashby the miller died in 1935, a year after the old mill had finally stopped; since then it has again been used for storage. In 1941 three enemy bombs destroyed the stables and some of the outbuildings; and it is on record that a pig, having been hurled through the roof, walked down Blenheim Gardens to the butcher's on the local Parade, and then, still dazed, into the Salvation Army hall, where it passed the rest of the night.

The Mill Cottage on the left dates from 1816; it backs on to a pleasant country-garden, full of bluebells and apple-trees, belonging to the Mill House, which is in the possession of the owner of the mill.

Queen Elizabeth had a house on Brixton Hill, which she visited by barge up the River Effra, then a real tributary of the Thames. Raleigh House (demolished about 1890) was not far away; and local belief insists that an underground passage led from it to the Queen's resort. It is a fact that some seventy years ago, boys at play found parts of an arched subway in that direction. Another local tradition is that the old elm still standing in Josephine Avenue, a few minutes walk from the Old Mill, was the tree under which Raleigh sat smoking the tobacco leaf he had brought back from the Americas, when his servant thought he was on fire and threw a bucket of water over him.

The Plate opposite is from a water-colour by G. L. Frost.

LONDON: SOUTHWARD AND EASTWARD

S T. THOMAS'S STREET, SOUTHWARK, is a street of mixed outline but persistent character, with little traffic except to Guy's Hospital. Its main charm comes from the iron gates to the forecourt enclosing the statue of Thomas Guy, bookseller-founder of the Hospital; Southwark Cathedral's Chapter House, with its Italianate tower, in the foreground of the picture; and (also in the picture) a terrace of pleasant Queen Anne houses, now professional offices, which escaped the bombs that blasted a wing of Guy's. The side opposite is Victorian: solid, grimy buildings facing a few average shops on the way to Borough High Street and the cathedral itself. John Keats, while he was a medical student at Guy's, shared lodgings in 1814–1815 over a tallow-chandler's shop in St. Thomas's Street with George Cooper, dresser to Sir Astley Cooper, the famous surgeon who befriended the young poet.

The Chapter House, built in 1702 as the church of St. Thomas, was mainly paid for (like St. Paul's) by a duty on coal. It is a relic of the second of the two great hospitals which once lay within the parish: this was the old monastic St. Thomas's Hospital, which, founded in 1213 as an almshouse, was bought by the citizens of London during the Dissolution of the Monasteries and was opened in 1552 as a hospital for the poor. The crypt of the church is said to have been used as the hospital's operating-theatre; and in part of it, still known as the Coffin Crypt, coffins were stored in case of need. The parents of the diarist John Evelyn were married in the church.

St. Thomas's was closed as a church by the Bishop of Southwark in August 1898, the congregation having so dwindled that the collection at the last service was only 3s. 6d. Until the war of 1939–1945 the Chapter House was headquarters for the Guild of Brave Poor Things—a name taken from Mrs. Ewing's book about a cripple, *The Story of a Short Life*. Cripples of all ages crowded St. Thomas's Street on Thursday afternoons, the blind led by their friends, the badly lame pushed in chairs to the Chapter House. Red was dominant in the waistcoats and shawls of the old people, who had learned to regard themselves as soldiers of fate. This Guild was the forerunner of the Heritage Craft Schools for cripples, now at Chailey in Sussex.

Plate 35 opposite is from a water-colour by Randolph Schwabe.

St. Thomas's Street

R. Schwabe 1934

THE SIGNWRITERS' SHOP, SOUTHWARK : Signwriting is a highly skilled trade which, before the late war, required about seven years of apprenticeship. Much pride in their craft animates the signwriters who work for the Anchor Brewery on inn-signs and the rest, in one of the most pictorial workshops of its kind in London. One of to-day's craftsmen has been forty years in the shop ; another, thirty-three years. The jobs bring plenty of contrast : painted lettering six feet high alternates with delicate quarter-inch brushwork or with the manipulation of gold-leaf.

The management helps to promote the traditions of the craft with its gallery of good work from the past. The century-old sign with a gold background, seen top-right in the picture (' Special Old Blended Scotch & Irish Whiskies and Very Choice Pale & Brown Brandies ') is painted on glass and must have taken a man six months to complete. The portrait on the facing wall is of Charles Herring (nephew of the noted racehorse-painter and coach-driver John Herring), who was manager of the Signwriters' Shop in the 1850's. It was he who placed in position the tablet above his portrait, as a memorial to Hudson Gurney, antiquary, verse-writer and M.P. (1775–1864), a director of the brewery and head of the wealthy Norfolk family of Gurneys, who left a legacy for the benefit of fifty employees.

The Anchor Brewery itself may have supplied the Southwark ale referred to by Chaucer. Its written records date from 1690. In the eighteenth century it was owned by the Thrale family, through whom Dr. Johnson became associated with the firm, being given a room of his own at the brewery, where he did his literary work (Johnson's head is the present trade-mark). Johnson was executor and trustee under Henry Thrale's will, in the interests of his friend Mrs. Thrale. He was very active when the sale of the property was decided upon, ' bustling about ' (Boswell reports Lord Lucan as saying) ' with a inkhorn and pen in his button-hole like an exciseman.' On the question of price he coined a standard phrase by proclaiming : ' We are not here to sell a parcel of boilers and vats, but the potentiality of wealth beyond the dreams of avarice.'

The purchaser of the brewery was David Barclay, Quaker director of Barclay's Bank ; and Thrale's manager, John Perkins, was also given a share in the business, which was founded as Barclay Perkins & Co. in 1781. The brewery was visited by many celebrities including the Prince Consort, Edward VII when Prince of Wales, Napoleon III and Bismarck. There occurred in 1850 an incident that caused diplomatic complications and a reprimand from Queen Victoria to Palmerston, who threatened resignation. The Austrian General Haynau, notorious for his brutalities in Hungary and Italy, was recognised after he had signed the Visitors' Book, and was chased by an angry crowd of labourers into a public-house. Garibaldi, when he came to London in 1864, asked to see the ' *fabrique de bière* ' where ' the men flogged Haynau ' ; and he toasted in the brewery's best beer the workmen of the world.

The Plate opposite is from a water-colour by Kenneth Rowntree.

BOW CHURCH, CHEAPSIDE : The German bombs which, on a May night in 1941, destroyed all but the walls, the crypt and the steeple of St. Mary-le-Bow Church, rendered one service to the London panorama : by clearing the foreground they opened an excellent view of Wren's complete elevation for this most famous of City churches (built in 1678–1679). A temporary chapel erected on the site of the ruined vestry conforms as nearly as possible to the church's structure. The superb steeple, 225 feet from ground-level, is topped by a dragon-vane nearly nine feet long. The balcony in the tower over the Doric entrance to the church was intended by Christopher Wren to commemorate an ornate stone building called the Crown Sild, from which medieval sovereigns watched the joustings in Cheapside.

St. Mary-le-Bow is believed to be so named from the ' bows ' or arches in the crypt of the original Norman church on the site (Roman bricks can still be seen, built into the crypt's walls). The roof of the early Norman building was blown off in 1090, but a second church lasted until it was burned down in the Great Fire. St. Mary-le-Bow, in all its phases, was one of the thirteen City churches that belonged to the diocese of Canterbury, instead of London, and were therefore called ' peculiars.' From the twelfth century until the bombing of 1941, the Court of Arches, the highest court of the Archbishop of Canterbury, sat within the altar rail. Pepys mentions a visit ' to Bow Church, to the Court of Arches, where a judge sits and his proctors about him in their habits, and their pleadings all in Latin.' Here newly appointed bishops in the Province of Canterbury took the oath of allegiance before enthronement in their own cathedrals. The Court now meets at Church House, Westminster.

The chimes of Bow Bells have been part of City lore ever since a legend, originating early in the sixteenth century, told how they turned back the fourteenth-century Dick Whittington to his destiny as Lord Mayor of London. Under the Plantagenets and Tudors, curfew was rung by Bow Bells each evening, after which none might be around in the City streets and no tavern might remain open. The claim that the true Londoner must have been born within sound of Bow Bells was invented by the City residents later, when London had spread outward to Westminster and beyond.

The original six bells were victims with their church in the Great Fire. A new set of eight were cast for Wren's building : a set of ten replaced these in time to be first rung on George III's twenty-fifth birthday. Two more bells were added to the top of the scale in the late nineteenth century ; and the full peal continued to be rung by bell-ringers drawn from the Ancient Society of College Youths. The chimes have survived the bells' destruction by enemy action : they can still be heard in a recording made before the war by the B.B.C.

In the foreground of the picture is the ruined Bread Street, in which Milton was born in 1608, and in which his father practised as a scrivener.

BOW CHURCH, CHEAPSIDE

REGINALD RILEY

PETTICOAT LANE, WHITECHAPEL : The address on Ministerial forms is Middlesex Street, E.1, but the name that belonged to it until fifty years ago remains in popular use. Petticoat Lane is too apt a name to be lost by the Street of the Sunday Market, where nearly three hundred stall-holders gather to sell at bargain prices all kinds of second-hand clothes, together with bedding, cheap jewellery, leather or imitation leather goods, ironmongery, perfumes and toilet knicknacks, ornaments for the parlour, musical instruments and many objects of variegated virtue.

In the time of John Stow, the Elizabethan chronicler and antiquary, it was called Hog Lane and was (he writes in 1598) in pleasant fields ' very commodious for citizens therein to walk, shoot and otherwise to recreate and refresh their dull spirits in the sweet and wholesome air ' ; but he goes on to lament that within a few years it was ' made a continual building throughout of garden houses and small cottages ; and the fields on either side be turned into garden plots, tenter-yards, bowling-alleys and such like.' The seventeenth-century historian John Strype refers to ' Petticoat Lane, formerly called Hog Lane.' Meanwhile some Huguenots, escaped from Catholic France, had founded ' in that part of the lane nearest Spittlefields' the colony of weavers whose skill was so beneficial to English industry. Ben Jonson in his play *The Devil is an Ass* makes Iniquity say :

> We will survey the suburbs, and make forth our sallies
> Down Petticoat Lane and up the smock-alleys.

During the week the traders search London and elsewhere for their stock. On Sunday morning, having arranged it in crowded display, they give it the benefit of loud, smart sales-talk. ' The Duchess of Windsor left this tablecloth behind when she went to America,' cries one. Others label themselves the Overcoat King, the Purse King, Mother Value or Captain Ki-Ki—Tools One Price Only. The stall-holders proper have their own trade-association, which frowns on illegality and demands that clothes-coupons be given when coupons are required. It is not exactly unknown for the cameras and things which men in the Army of Occupation bring back from Germany without formality of Customs, to be hawked at third-hand in Petticoat Lane ; but when this happens, the sellers are mostly unlicensed individualists who pick their customers as warily as they watch for the tactful City police.

The prices are at any rate reasonable. Before 1940, stockings could be had for a penny a pair, umbrellas for two shillings, afternoon dresses for five shillings, men's suits for twelve-and-six, near-fur coats for less than that, real fur ones for a guinea or two. Bargains of that kind have gone for ever, or until the next big slump ; but still, outside the few food-stalls (eels, shrimps, fruit and toffee-apples) the average of prices is barely half of what prevails in the suburban stores and second-hand shops. As for the buyers, they come from everywhere between Ilford and Highgate : Whitechapel may predominate, but cars come from St. John's Wood and Chelsea.

PETTICOAT LANE

RUPERT SHEPHARD

CLERKENWELL GREEN persists in clear-cut charm, though the residential glory has departed and humdrum buildings are used for the wares of metal-polishers, chemical glass-blowers, manufacturers of spaghetti and macaroni, and various small shops. The Green is a paved oblong ; as Dickens noted when he described how Oliver Twist, having watched Charley Bates and the Dodger pick the pocket of an old gentleman in a bottle-green coat and white trousers, suddenly realised the import of Fagin's lessons, took to his heels and was caught.

St. James's Church, in the background, is on the site of a former nunnery of the Benedictines : it was rebuilt in 1788-1791 by James Carr, who imitated a Wren steeple. Its galleried interior has at the west end a second gallery on delicate pillars. Buried in the churchyard is Thomas Britton, 'the musical small-coal man,' who in the late seventeenth century organised, in a low room over his coal-shed, weekly chamber-concerts to which Society flocked and at which Handel sometimes played.

The name Clerkenwell comes from the Clerks' Well where in medieval times the parish clerks performed miracle-plays. Near the Green was the Red Bull theatre of the Elizabethan actor-manager Edward Alleyn (Burbage's rival but Shakespeare's friend), who founded Dulwich College. The Priory of the Order of the Hospital of St. John of Jerusalem extended to the Green from the battlemented gate-house, dating from about 1504, which spans St. John's Lane to the south-east.

Clerkenwell, in the sixteenth and seventeenth centuries, was a fashionable area. Around the winding Close, seen leading out of the Green on the right of the picture, lived Sir Thomas Chaloner, Queen Elizabeth's Ambassador to Germany ; the Earl of Clanricarde ; Oliver Cromwell, at whose house the death-warrant of Charles I is said to have been signed ; an Earl of Exeter who in 1629 successfully objected to a brewhouse and forge which were causing damage to his dining-room by the smoke and to his nostrils by the smell ; and the Dukes of Newcastle, at whose mansion Pepys and Evelyn dined. Izaak Walton was living by the Green when he finished *The Compleat Angler*.

On the site now occupied by an L.C.C. school north of the Close stood the old Clerkenwell Bridewell (later known as the New Prison), in which many priests were imprisoned during the anti-Popery persecutions of the seventeenth century, as was the celebrated robber Jack Sheppard, who escaped from it in 1724. After enlargement, the building was used as a House of Detention for prisoners awaiting trial. A devastating explosion occurred in 1867 when a Fenian fired a barrel of gunpowder against the wall in an attempt to release arrested comrades.

CLERKENWELL GREEN   RANDOLPH SCHWABE

Plate 40

A LONDON ROOFSCAPE: VIEW FROM SOUTHWARK CATHEDRAL

HANSLIP FLETCHER

THE roofscapes of London are dun, grey, dark red and a smoky brown which, alone in the mists, changes hardly at all when sunshine lightens the pattern. Mr. Hanslip Fletcher's drawing, made from the tower of Southwark Cathedral (the nave of which briefly juts into his foreground), gives a westward vista from the Houses of Parliament on the left to St. Paul's on the right.

On the right of the artist's panorama, beyond the railway bridge leading to Cannon Street Station, is Southwark Bridge, opened in 1921 by George V. In the foreground is the Borough Market for fruit and vegetables. It adjoins Clink Street, the familiar name of which recalls the prison where many heretics were confined. This area, known as the Liberty of the Clink, was an entertainment-park in the sixteenth century, and earned ill repute; but dramatic performances flourished, and a company of actors played so close to St. Saviour's Church that their voices could be heard by the congregation while Stephen Gardiner, Bishop of Winchester and Chancellor of England, was saying Mass for Henry VIII's soul.

The diocese of Southwark dates from 1905, when that of Rochester was split up. The church, which thus became a cathedral, was originally founded by nuns in 606 as St. Mary Overy's. The Augustinian Canons erected a later church here in 1106, and, after its loss by fire a century later, rebuilt it in Gothic style as St. Saviour's. It gradually fell into disrepair during the seventeenth and eighteenth centuries; and the present building is largely a nineteenth-century reconstruction. In the nave, almost opposite to the tomb of the poet John Gower, Chaucer's friend, is the well-known Shakespeare Memorial. The cathedral's Shakespearean associations are carefully fostered, for near-by is the site of the Globe Theatre. Shakespeare himself lived in the parish from 1595 to 1611, and was almost certainly present at the burial of his brother Edmund (described in the records as 'a player') in 1607. In that same year John Harvard, later to be principal founder of the American University that bears his name, was baptised in the church, his father (a butcher) being a churchwarden. The memorial Harvard Chapel, built in 1907 by American subscription, opens out of the north transept.

GREENWICH : On a July day in 1763 Dr. Johnson and James Boswell
'took a sculler at the Temple-stairs, and set out for Greenwich,' where
Johnson had lived in apartments after his first departure from Lichfield.
Arrived there, Boswell declaimed Johnson's lines :

> On Thames's banks in silent thought we stood :
> Where Greenwich smiles upon the silver flood.
> Pleas'd with the seat which gave Eliza birth,
> We kneel, and kiss the consecrated earth.

Greenwich is a highly individual borough amid the massed, rather grim
acres of dockside. For centuries it was a place of royal pleasure, as well as a
shipping-centre. Greenwich Palace, on the site of the two domed buildings
in Mr. Claude Muncaster's vista, was made into a fortress by Humphrey,
Duke of Gloucester, the Regent during Henry VI's minority, to guard both
the river entry to London and the Roman road from Dover to Westminster ;
and, stocking it with books and *objets d'art*, he called it Bella Court. Margaret
of Anjou changed its name to Placentia. Henry VIII and his daughters Mary
and Elizabeth were born there. Queen Elizabeth said of the palace : 'Sure
the house, garden and walks may compare with any delicat place in Italy.'
Tradition makes it the scene of Raleigh's gallantry with his cloak.

The muddy Deptford-Woolwich road ran along the southern side of the
palace. In 1617 James I instructed Inigo Jones to demolish the Tudor gate-
house and erect instead a house for the Queen that should enable its inmates
to pass dryshod and in seclusion from the walled palace gardens to the park
slopes to the south. Thus arose, above the road, the remarkable Queen's
House, front centre in the picture. The buildings at each end form the National
Maritime Museum, where Nelson relics are housed. Charles II demolished
the palace and commissioned John Webb to build a new one ; but William
and Mary preferred Hampton Court to Greenwich, and it was Mary's idea
that the rising structure, redesigned by Wren, should form a hospital for
disabled seamen. The whole group of buildings is now the Royal Naval
College. In the domed block on the left is the magnificent Painted Hall,
with ceilings, walls and pillars painted by Sir James Thornhill. The State
dinner to the 214 delegates of the United Nations took place here in January,
1946. The corresponding block on the right contains the chapel.

The shipping at Greenwich developed in Elizabethan times and rose to its
peak of prosperity in the nineteenth century, when the London-Greenwich
railway (opened 1836) was the first line constructed in the metropolis. The
Royal Observatory, erected in 1675 to Wren's design for Flamsteed, the
first Astronomer-Royal, is on the hill from which the picture was painted.

GREENWICH FROM THE ROYAL OBSERVATORY

CLAUDE MUNCASTER

HORSELYDOWN LANE, BERMONDSEY

MONA MOORE

HORSELYDOWN LANE, BERMONDSEY, on the south bank of the Thames adjoining the Bermondsey end of Tower Bridge, is a narrow thoroughfare given over to Courage's Anchor Brewhouse, which has bridges connecting the buildings on either side of Horselydown (named Horseye Down in medieval times from the horses that were pastured and sold there). On the Roman road leading to the ferry across the Thames Sir John Fastolf, early in the fifteenth century, had his mansion, which he strongly garrisoned against Jack Cade's rebels. He had distinguished himself at Agincourt and was appointed Regent in Normandy and Governor of Anjou and Maine. There is a theory that Shakespeare intended his Falstaff to be a satiric portrait not (as is generally held) of Sir John Oldcastle, but of Fastolf; or he may have used a dramatist's licence to give some of Fastolf's well-known characteristics to his riotous knight. In the Tudor period Horselydown became a fair-ground; in 1544 the churchwardens of the parish were censured for not having provided archery butts as required by a statute of Henry VIII.

John Courage, of Huguenot descent, came to London from Aberdeen in the late eighteenth century to seek his fortune, and became agent for the Carron Line of London–Scottish coastal ships, whose wharf is still almost opposite the Courage brewery. The Carron Company, founded 1759, manufactured the famous ' carronade,' a short, large-bore cast-iron gun with which all their ships were armed until after the battle of Waterloo. The company's vessels could be recognised by a cannon-ball built into the main mast as an indication to friendly craft that these warlike traders were not French privateers : a distinctive black ball continues the custom to-day.

John Courage bought one of the four ' berehouses ' in Horselydown and built near it a brewery in the street known as Shad Thames (perhaps so named from the shoals of fish called shad that were then found locally in the Thames). His descendants extended the brewery until it became one of the best known in the world. In gas-lit Victorian times, the workers wore caps fitted in front with tallow candles, so as to see in the huge cellars the casks, which they filled singly through rubber hoses. The present brewery dates from the 1890's, the earlier buildings having been destroyed by a fire that for several days successfully defied the London Fire Brigade, which was helped by floats on the river and was led by the famous Captain Shaw mentioned in Gilbert's *Iolanthe*.

THE TOWER OF LONDON: ' I was all impatience to visit the Tower of London, of melodramatic fame. The historical monuments of this country, I notice, are popular in proportion to the horrors committed within their walls. Every self-respecting castle has a legend of bloodshed and murder.' So wrote the Frenchman Francis Wey, President of the *Société des Gens de Lettres*, in an entertaining account of his visit to England. That was in mid-Victorian times ; and it has been true of the Tower in all ages—doubly so in the sixteenth century, when scores of heads rolled on Tower Green within the fortress and on Tower Hill just outside it. The remains of thirty-four famous men and women from that century, including two of Henry VIII's queens (Anne Boleyn and Catherine Howard) and Lady Jane Grey lie within the Chapel of St. Peter ad Vincula, below the flagstaff in the picture. ' In truth,' wrote Macaulay, ' there is no sadder spot on earth than this little cemetery.'

Many distinguished prisoners were lodged in the Beauchamp Tower, on the right of Mr. Hanslip Fletcher's sketch (made from Tower Hill). Inscriptions carved on the walls by prisoners are still preserved, including one by Queen Elizabeth's Robert Dudley, Earl of Leicester, and another by Philip Howard, Earl of Arundel, who after ten years in custody died in 1595, still refusing to renounce Roman Catholicism. Among earlier captives in the Tower was the defeated Lancastrian, Henry VI, who there met his mysterious death in 1471. Thirteen years later, Edward IV's two sons, the Little Princes immortalised by Shakespeare, were universally believed to have been murdered, at the instance of Richard III, in the Bloody Tower (beyond the picture's scope). In our day enemy spies succeeded the bygone Captains and Kings for execution. The Tower is magnificent ; the Tower is historic. It is also a greater Madame Tussaud's, with atmosphere and authentic relics in place of waxworks.

The great square Norman Keep (the White Tower), which dominates the whole edifice, dates from the eleventh century. It was built on Roman foundations by Gundulf, Bishop of Rochester, for William the Conqueror. Its outer walls have immense thickness, varying from about 16 feet in the ground-level dungeons to 11 feet on the third floor. In the Council Chamber Richard II surrendered his throne to Henry IV in 1399. The oldest extant Norman church in England, the Chapel of St. John, with an austere, pillared nave at first-floor level, forms a small part of the Keep. The Crown Jewels attract gaping crowds.

An inner wall with thirteen towers encircles the Keep. This wall originally enclosed the domestic buildings built by the Norman and Plantagenet Kings to form a palace, which had a courtyard and a Great Hall built by Henry III. The palace became one of Oliver Cromwell's demolitions. An outer wall was added to the Tower by Edward I (a bastion damaged by German bombs can be seen left in the picture) : between it and the present steeply sloping gardens bounded by the railings of Tower Hill lies the wide moat, which after draining has become a ground for military sports and parades. The sentries at the Tower are furnished by a unit of Foot Guards ; stares of the visitors focus on the Yeomen Warders in Tudor uniforms, who act as highly articulate guides.

THE TOWER OF LONDON

HANSLIP FLETCHER

VIEW FROM TOWER BRIDGE : Even in summer so clear a Thames vista as this is infrequent. The artist's perch was on top of the tower of the brewery in Horselydown Lane, looking northward across the river

The trees of Tower Walk, the promenade fronting the Tower of London, are on the right of the picture. Below the Walk, at low tide, is a sandy beach which was opened to children through the efforts of the late Lord Wakefield, Constable of the Tower, and at the express wish of King George V. The battle-mented tower on the waterfront is above Traitors' Gate, through which prisoners passed on being brought by barge for confinement in the Tower.

On Tower Hill behind, where Sir Thomas More, the Earls of Essex and Strafford, Sir Thomas Wyatt, Archbishop Laud and the Duke of Monmouth were executed, rises the pyramidal tower of the Head Office of the Port of London Authority, designed by Sir Edwin Cooper. It is built on the site of the Navy Office where Pepys lived and worked as Secretary of the Navy Board. Another feature of Tower Hill is the burnt-out shell of Trinity House, erected in 1795, the Brethren of which (Mr. Winston Churchill often wears the uniform of an Elder Brother) supervise the licensing of pilots and the maintenance of lighthouses and buoys round the English coasts. The brick tower of All Hallows, Barking, the ancient church (now largely in ruins) in which William Penn was baptised and John Quincy Adams, sixth President of the United States was married, can be seen behind the left edge of the Tower Walk trees.

The black spire of St. Margaret Pattens, Eastcheap, rebuilt by Wren, rises above the buildings left of Tower Hill. Then comes, in the centre of the picture, the elegant white steeple on the Wren tower of St. Dunstan-in-the-East, to the right of the domed tower of the Coal Exchange (in its foundations a Roman bath and hypocaust were discovered). The early nineteenth-century Customs House, with its pillared façade, is prominent on the waterfront. Billingsgate Fish Market adjoins the Customs House on the left.

The south (Surrey) side of the river between Tower Bridge and London Bridge (in the left background) has twenty-five considerable wharves. In one of these the greatest fire since 1666 broke out in 1861 : warehouses by the river were burning for a quarter of a mile, the fire spread to ships filled with oil, tallow and tar, so that the Thames was literally ablaze, and James Braidwood, Superintendent of the Metropolitan Fire Brigade and the inventor of the first steam fire-engine, lost his life.

A tunnel runs under the Thames from Tower Hill to Tooley Street on the Surrey side, in the form of a cast-iron tube. It was opened in 1870, when passengers made the journey in a small car running on rails. Later the subway was open to pedestrians ; but when its usefulness ended with the building of Tower Bridge it was bought by the London Hydraulic Power Company, who installed their own mains and two belonging to the Metropolitan Water Board.

The Plate opposite is from a water-colour by Henry Rushbury, R.A.

THE ANCHOR TAVERN, BANKSIDE: 'Small, snug and trim, with little rooms and low ceilings; a village inn set in the heart and hum of London.' So the late Thomas Burke, a life-long enthusiast for his native London, described the old tavern at the corner of a wharf facing Cannon Street Station across the Thames. It is now shored up with timber to prevent collapse after the damage caused by bombs; but it still serves good beer to many. Behind it rise the tall chimneys of the Anchor Brewery. The seventeenth-century design of the small tavern delights the onlooker passing from the gloomy Victorian warehouses that overshadow the place from the west. The walls include cupboards that conceal secret staircases, which may have been used for hiding contraband spirits or escaped prisoners from the neighbouring 'Clink,' later burned down by 'No Popery' rioters.

The eastern windows overlook Park Street, formerly called Deadman's Place from the number of people buried there during the Plague. It was from a Bankside tavern (possibly the predecessor of the Anchor itself) that Samuel Pepys watched the Fire of London: 'When we could endure no more upon the water, we to a little alehouse on the Bankside . . . and there staid till it was dark almost, and saw the fire grow, and as it grew darker, appeared more and more, and in corners and upon steeples and between churches and houses, as far as we could see up the hill of the City, in a most horrid malicious bloody flame.'

The seventeenth-century tavern replaced an older one which Shakespeare, Beaumont and Fletcher, Ford, Webster and Massinger, and other of the great Elizabethan dramatists are said to have frequented. The belief derives from its nearness to Burbage's old Globe Theatre, the generally accepted site of which in Park Street is marked by a pictorial plaque from the Shakespeare Reading Society of London and from subscribers in the United Kingdom and India. A rival inscription, barely legible because of the neglect which is justified by inaccuracy, announces from the wall of a warehouse on the river front adjoining the Anchor Tavern: 'Here stood the Globe Playhouse of Shakespeare, 1613.'

The Plate opposite is from a water-colour by E. B. Musman.

LONDON RIVER

BUGSBY'S REACH: Nobody knows who Mr. Bugsby was. The anti-quarians of London River have failed to find him in any of the files, manuscripts or topographical records. Even the Port of London Authority, which is wise and efficient, cannot trace him. He may have been a market-gardener who threw his refuse into the river, or a marine-store dealer who, having piled up a heap of old iron on the river-bank, defied his creditors from this castle of junk. The reach that bears his name is between Blackwall Reach and Woolwich Reach, on the eastern side of one of the river's great bends. The picture was painted from a point near Brunswick Wharf.

The River Lea flows into the Thames by Bow Creek, at the beginning of Bugsby's Reach and close to Trinity House Wharf, the depot for the lighthouses, lightships and channel-marking buoys round the English coast. From Bugsby's Reach to Gallion's Point (three miles) there is the uninterrupted lane of the Royal Docks parallel with the river, providing eleven miles of deep-water quays and forming the largest enclosed area of dock-water in the world, forty miles from the seaward limit of the Port. The great Royal Victoria Dock, entered from Bugsby's Reach, deals chiefly with grain, fruit and chilled meat; on its south side are huge flour-mills, on the north side are warehouses which before the recent war contained a stock of tobacco valued at £50,000,000. This dock is linked to the Royal Albert Dock, which is connected to the south with the King George V Dock, where there are fourteen berths for liners of up to 30,000 net register tons.

It was from the neighbouring Blackwall Reach that in 1606 the 105 emigrants who colonised Virginia sailed in three ships: among them Captain John Smith, their future leader. On the same Reach J. M. W. Turner watched, one evening in 1838, the ship of the line *Téméraire* being towed up-river to be broken up in Rotherhithe: hence his inspiration for the famous picture of *The Fighting Téméraire* in the National Gallery.

In the centre of the picture is a Thames sailing-barge with russet sails. These craft, built to a design evolved from centuries of experience, are flat-bottomed and of shallow draught; they carry cargoes of bricks, cement and the like cheaply and economically. Skipper and mate comprise the crew, whose lives W. W. Jacobs made familiar to readers. Mr. H. M. Tomlinson, that admirable chronicler of London's river, wrote of them: 'The men who continued to tack those apparently unhandy craft about the Thames estuary, that maze of tides, currents and shoals, with minefields added, during the siege of London, and along the coast while trouble was everywhere and unpre-dictable, were seamen of the right sort.'

Plate 46 opposite is from a water-colour by John Pimlott.

THE ROYAL HOTEL, PURFLEET, was one of the 'whitebait inns' which drew custom down-river from London in the nineteenth century. Parnell and Kitty O'Shea are said to have visited it often in the 1880's, as did many theatrical people. Thousands of ex-soldiers in both World Wars remember the locality from their stay in the great transit camps at Purfleet which waited upon shipping at Tilbury docks, eastward along the coast.

The view in the painting looks up-river from the Essex shore, along the Erith Rands (the Anglo-Saxon word *rand* meant an edge or border, and in this connection denoted the existence of a shoal). In medieval times pilgrims from Essex to Canterbury crossed to the Kentish shore by ferry from the Mermaid Causeway, Purfleet. Records from the same period describe the capture in the same part of the estuary of creatures rarely seen in British waters : in 1457 four 'great fysshes' were caught — two whales, a walrus and a swordfish. Further antiquity is represented by several Dane Holes, or subterranean caves in the chalk, possibly the result of prehistoric flint-workings : one such tunnel is believed to extend a mile under the Thames.

The chalk cliffs (on which a lighthouse formerly stood) gave rise to a lime-burning industry ; and the chalk was formerly used as ship's ballast. Nowadays Purfleet's industries include a margarine factory, a cement works and a paper mill. In 1924 an illuminated tidal-gauge was erected at Purfleet, close to the channel used by shipping between Tilbury Dock and the Royal Albert Dock, so that pilots can note the correct level of the tide as they take their ships up- or down-river.

The Plate opposite is from a water-colour by Patrick Hall.

WOOLWICH, now best known for its arsenal and the football team, had its finest hour as a royal dockyard, building and conditioning Charles II's ships for the sea-battles of Blake and other admirals.   When London thought that the Dutch fleet would sail up the Thames, guns were placed there ; and ships were sunk as obstacles below Woolwich and Blackwall.   Samuel Pepys, as Secretary of the Navy Board, visited Woolwich often : through his energy in getting men from the dockyard to pull down buildings in the path of the Great Fire, he saved the Navy Office on Tower Hill.   During the plague that followed the Fire, he removed his family to Woolwich ; and in 1667 Mrs. Pepys went there for the night ' to gather May-dew to-morrow morning which Mrs. Turner hath taught her is the only thing in the world to wash her face with.'   Charles II also built at Woolwich the first small craft called ' yachts.'

The dockyard had been built under Henry VIII, who was as navy-minded as any English monarch.   Under Elizabeth the first four ships of the East India Company (granted a Charter on the last day of 1600) sailed from Woolwich in 1601, and returned two and a half years later with a cargo of 1,030,000 pounds of pepper.   James Lancaster, their senior captain, kept the men of his own ship in good health (the other ships lost 105 out of 278 men from scurvy) by dosing each with three spoonfuls of lemon-juice every morning : a preventive which was then forgotten as such for nearly two hundred years. From Woolwich, too, Martin Pring and Charles Leigh sailed in 1604, in the tiny *Olive Plant*, to colonise British Guiana.

Prison hulks were moored off Woolwich to house convicts working in the dockyard and arsenal.   The regulations provided that they should ' be fed with legs and shins of beef, ox-cheek and such other coarse food and to have nothing to drink but water or small beer.'   The dockyard, for the rest, belonged to the ages of wood and iron in shipbuilding : no sea-going vessels have been built there since 1870.

There was caught off Woolwich in 1642 a weird, toadlike creature ' with fingers like a man and chested like a man, near five feet long and three feet over the thickness of an ordinary man.'   It was exhibited at Westminster.

The stretch of river in the picture is called Woolwich Reach, which becomes Gallion's Reach somewhat further east.   The viewpoint is North Woolwich, the area of 500 acres north of the Thames which was given to the Sheriff of Kent at the Norman Conquest and continued to be part of Kent until the County of London came into being in 1888.   The free ferry in the foreground, with its paddle-steamers of queer shape, links North and South Woolwich ; and there is also a tunnel for pedestrians under the Thames.

WOOLWICH FROM THE ROYAL PAVILION HOTEL

PATRICK HALL

ROTHERHITHE'S old church of St. Mary's, the spire of which rises behind flour-mills in Mr. Adrian Bury's picture, was originally a medieval building, the district (known as Redrithe) having formed part of the ancient manor of Bermondsey. The church was rebuilt in 1715, with woodwork by Grinling Gibbons. It has many memorials of seafaring people : among them a seventeenth-century Captain, described as 'Landsmen's Counceller, Seamen's Glory, Schisme's Scourge and Truth's Liveing Story.' Another tablet, presented by the India Office, commemorates Lee Boo, son of the King of Coorooraa, one of the Pelew Islands in the Pacific Ocean, who died of smallpox in 1784 and was buried in the churchyard, having been invited to England when he and his people succoured the crew of the East India Company's wrecked vessel *Antelope*.

Rotherhithe built ships long before it became the chief yard for the East India Company. A 'Corporation of Free Shipwrights of England' or 'Foreign Shipwrights' arose there in 1605 to oppose the restrictive policy of the 'Free Shipwrights of London' and 'practise their trade in all rivers and ports.' The Howland Great Wet Dock, surrounded by trees to break the force of the wind, was in use in 1703, the first of its kind in London. In 1763 it was sold to a firm which adapted it for whalers and renamed it the Greenland Dock ; it was again sold in 1806, and later merged into the system of the Surrey Commercial Docks.

Pepys often walked over the fields between this district and the shipyards at Deptford, where Mrs. Bagwell, his 'Valentine,' conveniently lived : his Diary describes his junketings with this lady in a curious mixture of French and other foreign words. Occasionally he would stop for refreshment at Halfway House, where he played ninepins ; and at the riverside Cherry Garden, another place of entertainment standing near the present Cherry Garden Stairs, he would collect cherries to take home to his wife.

The Thames Tunnel, designed by Sir Marc Brunel and begun in 1825, goes under the river close to this part of Rotherhithe. A huge shield of twelve frames with thirty-six cells, in each of which a separate group of miners worked, was gradually forced onward as excavation progressed. The sensation caused by this feat of engineering was reflected in the many Tunnel 'peep-shows' that became the rage among early Victorian children, not only in England but also in France and Germany. Annual fairs, brilliantly illuminated, were held in the Tunnel ; in 1853 some 40,000 people attended the fair. Further to the east the Rotherhithe Tunnel, constructed by the London County Council and opened in 1908, runs obliquely under the Thames.

EVENING AT ROTHERHITHE

ADRIAN BURY

TOWER BRIDGE FROM WAPPING ENTRANCE :   Tower Bridge was built in 1886-1894, after the citizens of an ever-growing London had presented many petitions for a new crossing below London Bridge.   The final design for a bascule bridge was accepted from Sir Horace Jones, as architect, and Sir J. Wolfe-Barry, as engineer.   It was opened by the then Prince and Princess of Wales in June of 1894, when, according to *The Times:* ' Conditions were faultless.   Paris herself never saw a fairer sky, and the Seine never shone under a brighter sun than the Thames on Saturday.' Archbishop Benson and Mr. Asquith, as Home Secretary, were in attendance. It was recorded, however, that the loudest applause was given to Lord Leighton, President of the Royal Academy.

It is not the loveliest of bridges ; and this was recognised by *The Times* in a leading article : ' The Tower-bridge is one of the structural triumphs of this age of steel.   From top to bottom the real fabric is of metal, and the seemingly massive masonry has been added, we are told, for purely ornamental purposes.   Such a confession is in itself sufficient to condemn the work and its authors in the judgment of the more austere disciples of a well-known aesthetic school.   To veneer steel with granite must seem to them a wanton outrage against the first canons of their creed.   The Tower-bridge, it is to be feared, will in their eyes be one more black crime in the long list which they have drawn up against modern engineers.'   H. G. Wells likened the bridge to ' a stockbroker in armour.'

The Wapping Entrance is to the London Docks.   Close to the river, at this point, were the great breweries which in Elizabethan days supplied beer for the English armies in the Low Countries and for the fighting ships of Effingham and Drake.   Until the eighteenth century pirates were hanged at a spot near-by called Execution Dock, their bodies being fastened by a chain harness to a post at low water, and kept there while three tides flowed over them ; among such was Captain Kidd.   Nearly a whole parish was pulled down, and 11,300 inhabitants were moved, when the site for St. Katharine Docks (further toward Tower Bridge) was cleared in the 1820's.   Before the docks arose in the early nineteenth century, river robberies were frequent and ruffians swarmed over Wapping.   Until about 1850 the wharves and their taverns were toured by touts trying to sell passages to America, without any provision having been made for food on the voyage.

In Wapping High Street is the well-known Town of Ramsgate Inn (formerly the Red Cow), where in 1688 Bloody Jeffreys, the ' hanging judge,' was mobbed by a crowd who recognised him beneath his disguise as a common seaman : train-bands rescued and arrested him.   Nelson, on going to sea for the first time, bought his kit at a shop next door to the Town of Ramsgate. Neighbouring spice mills where ginger, cinnamon, pepper and the rest are ground by huge granite stones make the air fragrant in this part of Wapping.

CLAUDE MUNCASTER

TOWER BRIDGE FROM WAPPING ENTRANCE

Plate 51

A VISTA OF BRIDGES : Westward from Shell-Mex House Lambeth Bridge shows faintly
in the background beyond Westminster Bridge, which was built in 1861 to replace the
old stone bridge of 1750, and was partly financed by the proceeds of public lotteries (the
new bridge also had its gambling moment : Lord Randolph Churchill won a bet by running
right across it while Big Ben was striking midnight). Next are a temporary bridge and
Charing Cross (or Hungerford) bridge, as unlovely as lack of proportion can make it.

The dome on the right of the picture belongs to Central Hall, Westminster, where in January
of 1946 the delegates of the United Nations first met. Peeping above a spire of the block
called Whitehall Court is one of the western towers of Westminster Abbey. The buildings

FRANCES MACDONALD

further to the left are New Scotland Yard. Next come the Houses of Parliament, pinnacled neo-Gothic buildings that were started in 1840 to the design of Sir Charles Barry and his assistant Augustus Pugin after the burning of the old Parliament buildings in 1834. The Chamber of the House of Commons was destroyed by a German bomb in 1941, and is now being rebuilt within the same structure. Parliament's Clock Tower contains the great bell, weighing $13\frac{1}{2}$ tons, nicknamed Big Ben after Sir Benjamin Hall, a First Commissioner of Works. It was cast in Whitechapel, and was drawn to Westminster by sixteen white horses. Across the Thames are the seven detached blocks forming St. Thomas's Hospital. County Hall, to the left, was opened in 1923 as London's municipal parliament.

LONDON BRIDGE FROM BILLINGSGATE WHARF : London Bridge was until 1739 the only bridge across London's part of the Thames. There was a sequence of bridges on much the same site, including a Roman one and a Saxon one, which King Canute's invading ships by-passed through a canal dug on the Surrey side. The old song, 'London Bridge is Falling Down,' is said to derive from the time when Olaf of Norway allied himself with Ethelred the Unready, and broke down an ancient wooden bridge in an attack on the Danes (1014).

The medieval bridge, originally built in 1176-1209 and known as Old London Bridge, survived for centuries by virtue of many reconstructions. It had twenty arches (two were discovered on the north bank in 1921, when the foundations for the new Adelaide House were being sunk) ; a drawbridge in the middle and a gate-house at each end, where the heads of traitors were fixed on poles and exposed ; a chapel and crypt in the centre ; and a double row of houses and shops. Its booksellers and print-sellers were of high repute. The houses were interrupted by ' void spaces ' for passengers : Pepys records how, during the great storm of 1666, he and Lord Brouncker ' were fain to stoop very low for fear of blowing off the bridge.' Running underneath, or ' shooting the bridge,' had many dangers because of the narrowness of the arches, the cornmills obstructing some of the openings, and the water-works built at the southern end in 1582. There was a five-foot drop when the tide ran, and in the early eighteenth century jumping overboard became a fashionable form of suicide. ' London Bridge,' wrote Ray in 1738, ' was made for wise men to go over and fools to go under.'

The present bridge, designed by John Rennie and built by his son Sir John Rennie, was opened in 1831 by William IV, who with Queen Adelaide went to it by water from Westminster. A pavilion was erected on the bridge, for a banquet given to the King by the Lord Mayor and City Corporation.

Billingsgate has been a market for fish dealers ever since it was a Saxon port. The Thames fishing was lucrative in Plantagenet and Tudor times, when salmon persisted in the river (Henry VIII's polar bear was taken on expeditions from the Tower to fish for salmon) ; the last salmon caught in the Thames was in 1833. The wharf is of great antiquity ; during hundreds of years it was used to accommodate fleets of fishing vessels from Faversham, Rochester, Colchester, Dover and other seaports. Billingsgate has since become more than a fish-centre, and ships up to 1,000 tons register come up the river to lie at the wharf. The stretch of river from London Bridge to Limehouse Reach is known as the Pool of London.

LONDON BRIDGE FROM BILLINGSGATE WHARF

PATRICK HALL

ST. PAUL'S FROM BANKSIDE

S. DENNANT MOSS

ST. PAUL'S, FROM BANKSIDE : It was from vantage-points in Bankside, across the river, that Sir Christopher Wren watched the rising of his great cathedral. He had been summoned from Oxford in 1668 to report as surveyor-general and principal architect for rebuilding the whole City, the cathedral church of St. Paul's, all the parochial churches and other public structures. Much to his disappointment, his original and favourite design for the cathedral was declined, owing partly to opposition from clerics who disliked the plan of a Greek cross and the absence of side-chapels. A revised design was accepted in 1675 ; the choir of the cathedral was opened for service in 1697 ; and the last stone was laid in 1710. Wren fell into disfavour soon after the accession of George I and was superseded before he could carry out the finishing touches ; but it is unexampled for so vast a cathedral to have been completed within the lifetime of the man who designed it and oversaw the entire construction.

This view of the dome shows how very well Wren carried out the instruction that it must be ' conspicuous above the houses ' : in his day no City roof rose higher than forty feet above the street. Turner once said that the dome *made* London. Observed from the exterior as a magnificent landmark, it is not the same dome as that seen from inside the cathedral. Problems of architecture required a double shell, as in the Pantheon at Rome. The interior cupola, fashioned in brick, is fifty feet lower than the exterior dome, which is made of wood with a lead covering. The great cross and lantern (together, they weigh 700 to 800 tons) rest on an intermediate cone of brickwork between the dome and the interior cupola. The summit of the cross is about 365 feet above the ground. During the big fires in the City that were caused by enemy bombing in 1940–1941, the cross shone as an inspiration to firemen and rescue-squads amid the glare of flames and searchlights. Halfway down, above the peristyle or colonnade, is a balustraded gallery from which on a fine day all London can be seen.

An alarming crack appeared in the dome in 1925. A National Fund to finance the immediate repair demanded by the three trustees of St. Paul's (the Primate, the Bishop of London and the Lord Mayor) brought £230,000 in contributions that ranged from thousands of pounds to one shilling ' from thirteen loyal Scots.' Two chains of stainless steel, each weighing some thirty tons, now encircle the drum below the Whispering Gallery, to prevent expansion in hot weather.

Bankside, the earliest of the Thames embankments, was a noted pleasure-haunt in the Tudor and Stuart periods. The Bankside of those days is recalled by such names, amid the present wharves and warehouses, as Paris Garden, Bear Garden and Rose Alley. Under Elizabeth and James I, the stews and taverns of Bankside were notorious. Further along toward Southwark were the Globe Theatre and the prison of the Clink.

KING'S REACH: VIEW FROM SHELL-MEX HOUSE. The southern vista stretches from Westminster Bridge, on the distant right, to Tower Bridge on the left, and takes in the stretch of river named King's Reach since George V's Silver Jubilee in 1935. The Surrey-Kent suburban districts are in the background. County Hall is on the river-bank to the extreme right. In the centre is the mass of Waterloo Station : the original station of 1848 had 3 platforms and 14 trains a day ; the present station (opened in 1922) has 22 platforms and more than 1,200 trains a day. On the river-bank fronting the station is the Shot Tower, dating from William IV's reign, where shot was made by pouring molten lead through a perforated platform on top of the tower into a tank of water below. The campanile tower on the extreme left is on the Oxo Company's building. A fine new embankment stretching from County Hall to Southwark Cathedral is now in the hands of the London County Council's planners.

Spanning the river left of the Shot Tower is the new Waterloo Bridge, which was opened for six lines of traffic in 1944, after seven years of work. The bridge it replaced was an acknowledged masterpiece by John Rennie, opened in 1817, on the anniversary of the Battle of Waterloo, by the Prince Regent in the presence of the Duke of Wellington. Originally burdened with tolls, it became a free bridge in 1878 (tolls were removed from all bridges below Battersea in 1879) ; its demolition was decided by the London County Council because of a subsidence in one of the piers.

Cleopatra's Needle stands high in the foreground on the Victoria Embankment, north of the river. This obelisk, originally set up in front of the temple of Heliopolis by Thotmes III of Egypt nearly 3,500 years ago, was removed by Cleopatra in *c.* 14 B.C. to Alexandria, where for centuries it lay half-covered with sand, until Mohamed Ali presented it to Britain in 1820. It stayed prostrate in the sand for a further fifty-seven years ; after which Sir Erasmus Wilson gave £10,000 to cover the cost of transport to England. A special cylindrical boat, the *Cleopatra*, was built to carry the obelisk : but storms in the Bay of Biscay caused the boat to break away from the ship towing it, and it was abandoned after six lives had been lost. The boat was later taken in tow by a passing steamer, and reached London in 1878, when the much-harried obelisk was erected on the Thames Embankment. Beneath the foundation-stone were buried a number of typical objects of the 1870's, including a shilling razor, a feeding-bottle and a box of hairpins.

The Victoria Embankment itself was constructed by Sir Joseph Bazalgette in the 1860's, on what had been a muddy foreshore at low tide ; and it was opened with emphatic pomp by Edward, Prince of Wales. The picture on the facing page was painted from Shell-Mex House, built on the former site of the Hotel Cecil, which in the pre-Ritz era of 1870 to 1900 was considered one of the most splendid hotels ever.

KING'S REACH : VIEW FROM SHELL-MEX HOUSE

FRANCES MACDONALD

THE RUTLAND HOTEL, HAMMERSMITH, which gives a first-class view of the annual Boat-race between Oxford and Cambridge as the rival boats arrive from Putney, shoot under Hammersmith Bridge and then curve round the river bend toward Barnes and the finishing-post at Mortlake, has much else to do with rowing. Though damaged by bomb-blast in the late war, it is still a rowing house and the headquarters of well-known rowing clubs. Behind are the sheds where George Sims has built half a dozen University boats since Oxford broke the succession of thirteen Cambridge victories in 1937. From a spot near the Rutland, Walter Greaves, Whistler's boatman and assistant who became an artist in his own right, must have made sketches for his painting of Hammersmith Bridge crowded with Boat-race spectators in the Tate Gallery's well-known picture.

The present bridge, designed by Sir Joseph Bazalgette and opened in 1887 by the Duke of Clarence, replaced an earlier suspension-bridge (the first of its kind in London) which had been inaugurated in 1827 amid much excitement and many fireworks. Mendelssohn, then in his twentieth year, describes a drive over the earlier bridge in a cabriolet.

The hotel stands on the Lower Mall between Hammersmith and Chiswick. This and the Upper Mall were fashionable from the seventeenth to the early nineteenth century. Sir Samuel Morland, the famous mechanic who invented water-pumps, the capstan, a speaking-trumpet and a form of Braille, lived on the Lower Mall. When John Evelyn visited him here, Sir Samuel, who was then blind, said he had newly buried £200 worth of music-books in the garden, ' they being all love songs and vanity.' Nearby a board on an old holly-tree marks the space where Nell Gwyn's house, West Lodge, stood until German bombs demolished it.

The ancient village of Hamoders Hithe stood beside a creek dividing Lower from Upper Malls : the creek was cemented over in the 1930's as part of the plan for the new Town Hall set back from the river-front. Beyond the creek and the sometime ghost-haunted alley called Hampshire Hog Lane are Sussex House, where William Morris printed his Kelmscott *Chaucer*, and Kelmscott House, where Morris lived at the time (' I don't fancy going back among the bugs of Bloomsbury,' he wrote to his wife), and where Sir Francis Ronalds had in 1816 constructed the first electric telegraph, eight miles long. A plaque on a neighbouring house recalls the Doves Bindery of Cobden-Sanderson, Morris's follower, who first used the term ' Arts and Crafts.'

The Upper Mall has two curving bastions over the river : these were made to allow coaches to turn in the roadway when visiting Charles II's widow, Catherine of Braganza. Dr. John Radcliffe, William III's witty physician, whose fortune provided the funds for the Library, Infirmary and Observatory at Oxford that bear his name, was a later tenant of the Queen's house.

The Plate opposite is from a water-colour by Ruskin Spear.

HAMPTON COURT BRIDGE, designed by Sir Edwin Lutyens, spans the Thames to East Molesey, which has the second longest lock on the river (the longest being Teddington). Hampton Court, with its famous Palace, its nearness to Bushy Park and its pleasant river-side inns (including the well-known Mitre), is peer to Richmond among the Thames resorts near London. With the quieter upstream village of Hampton it is also a starting-point for Londoners who undertake river holidays on the lines of *Three Men in a Boat* or, what is more frequent nowadays, Two Girls in a Punt.

The Palace, an architectural symphony in various shades of red, has its main entrance through the Trophy Gates a few yards from the bridge on the Middlesex side. For nearly 250 years Hampton Court was a royal residence: twelve successive sovereigns of England lived there, from Henry VIII to George II. The original palace was begun in 1514 by Cardinal Wolsey, who entertained in it the French Ambassador's 400-strong retinue when confirming the agreement between France and England known as the Treaty of Hampton Court. Wolsey presented the Palace to Henry VIII, who built the Great Hall and Tennis Court, gave the Chapel Royal its splendid vaulting and added many State rooms. Catherine Howard and Catherine Parr were each married to Henry in the Palace. Catherine Howard's shrieking ghost is said still to haunt the gallery down which, her misconduct discovered, she ran to appeal to the King when he was at Mass in his Oratory. Anne Boleyn passed her honeymoon at Hampton Court; Jane Seymour died there twelve days after giving birth to the child who was to be Edward VI. Queen Mary Tudor, after her marriage to Philip of Spain, awaited in the palace the confinement that never came, though letters in French headed ' Hampton Court 1555 ' and addressed to all the Sovereigns of Europe were ready to announce the child's birth. Queen Elizabeth, whose reconciliation with her sister Mary had taken place at Hampton Court, stayed frequently in the Palace. Shakespeare played his *Henry VIII* in the Great Hall at Christmas 1603 before James I, who next month presided over the Hampton Court Conference which decided on the compilation of the Authorised Version of the Bible. Charles I and Cromwell used the Palace; Charles II revived its earlier splendours.

Then came Wren's great rebuilding for William and Mary, who wanted a rival to Versailles; the Fountain Court, the superb south and east fronts, and the elegant gardens date from this period. The first two Georges lived frequently at the Palace; George II, when Prince of Wales, established a sort of Court in it. George III, perhaps with unpleasant memories of having his ears boxed by his grandfather there, ended Royalty's close association with Hampton Court; and a thousand rooms were gradually converted into apartments for needy aristocrats and widows and children of distinguished servants of the Crown. The State Apartments contain many famous pictures by Old Masters.

The Plate opposite is from a water-colour by Rupert Shephard.

HOME COUNTIES: NORTHWARD

THE CAMPUS, WELWYN GARDEN CITY: This flourishing experiment in rural urbanity rose from the vision of a young man named Ebenezer Howard, son of a confectioner in the City of London. Being strongly influenced by Emerson, Lowell and other unsectarian thinkers in the United States, where he had lived for five years, he developed during further years, while working as a shorthand-writer in the Houses of Parliament, the idea of a new civilisation based on service to the Community. In 1898 he wote a book which was reissued four years later under the title *Garden Cities of To-morrow*: in this he put forward his plan to remedy the overcrowding and slum-conditions of large cities by building new towns within rural belts. He called these ' garden cities '; and an essential feature was that each town should own its land.

Sir Ebenezer Howard thus began the movement which in 1903 developed at Letchworth in Hertfordshire. In 1919 the association that planned it under Howard's presidency bought the agricultural estate at Welwyn, ten miles away, which after some critical years grew into the self-contained township of Welwyn Garden City. The International Garden Cities and Town Planning Association has exercised a beneficent influence on urban development all over the world. The Abercrombie Plan for Greater London, adopted by the British Government in 1945, named Welwyn Garden City as the prototype on which ten new satellite towns were to be modelled.

The town's administration is divided between an Urban Council and the Welwyn Garden City Company, as sole landowner. Particular pride is taken in the upkeep of the trees, shrubs and gardens that line most of the roads. The central Campus in the picture is one of many open spaces and playgrounds in and around the rapidly expanding town. Some eighty industrial firms have been attracted to Welwyn: many of them have erected well-designed factories in keeping with the pleasant houses that cater for every section of the community. The town's inhabitants increased by fifty per cent in 1939-1940, when 20,000 people were living there. The enormous Company-owned department-store overlooking the Campus, completed at a cost of over £250,000 only two months before the declaration of war, helped to fulfil their growing needs and justified the wisdom of its designers.

Plate 57 opposite is from a water-colour by A. R. Whitear.

Michael Kollwostein

THE MALTINGS, SAWBRIDGEWORTH, HERTS : These stand in the valley of the little River Stort. On the hill is the largish village of Sawbridgeworth, lying between Harlow and Bishop's Stortford near the Essex border. At right angles to the main road, Bell Street, with its old timbered and pargeted houses, leads to Sawbridgeworth Church, which is unusually rich in brasses and monuments, chiefly of the two families of Joscelyn and Leventhorp. A Ralph Joscelyn was twice Lord Mayor of London in the fifteenth century ; a Sir John Leventhorp, commemorated by a large and striking brass, was an executor of Henry V's will.

The Taylor family have been interested in the malting industry in this area for over 150 years, and some of their up-to-date maltings are here.

Few drinkers of beer—'mild,' 'bitter,' 'brown' or 'pale'—know the processes that the ingredients undergo before they reach the bottle or the barrel. The colour and flavour of ales are determined by the different kinds of malt used. The barley, from which all foreign matter has been removed, is steeped in water in cisterns and then spread on tiled floors or put in drums, where it is carefully turned for about ten days while it germinates. Air-conditioning plants now enable the temperature to be controlled throughout the year, whereas formerly malting could be done satisfactorily only from September to May. The malt is dried off in kilns. The 'culms' which the grain sheds during the process of forced growth are sold as cattle food.

A separate factory produces malt extract, which in syrup and powder form has many uses in the modern world : by bakers, as a yeast food to ensure good fermentation and improved bread with better keeping qualities ; by pharmacists, who buy it plain in syrup form and in combination with cod liver oil and vitamin products ; by patent-food manufacturers, in combination with milk, cocoa, and eggs, and for malted breakfast foods ; by brewers, to improve the quality of their beer. Many tons of malt extract go to cotton mills, which use it to remove the dressing from fabrics leaving the looms, before the patterns are printed on them. Laundries, too, use it to remove the starch from collars and other articles of clothing before washing.

The Plate opposite is from a water-colour by Michael Rothenstein.

FRENCH ROW, ST. ALBANS : This ancient, unobtrusive city derives its name from the first Christian martyr of Britain, a Roman soldier called Albanus who was executed in A.D. 303 for sheltering a priest and adopting Christianity. St. Albans was the Verulamium of the Romans. Julius Cæsar had captured the place in 54 B.C., when it was the headquarters of the British chieftain Cassivelaunus ; and it later became an important centre of the Roman occupation (the theatre and other well-preserved remains are guide-book attractions). The Romano-British inhabitants were overwhelmed in A.D. 61 by Boadicea, Queen of the Iceni tribes. A monastery in memory of Albanus was established in 793. The great abbey-church, the nave of which is the longest in England, took shape in the eleventh century, being built largely with red bricks collected from the ruins of Roman Verulamium. The representative Council that discussed King John's promise to make amends for his misbehaviour met at St. Albans in 1213. The third printing-press in England was set up here about 1479 ; and printing is still one of the town's major industries.

French Row is a pleasant, narrow street lined with small shops and leading from the bustling Market Place to the main London road. Toward its far end on the right is the Fleur de Lys inn, forming part of a house in which Jean le Bon, King of France, is believed to have been held captive for a time when awaiting ransom after the battle of Poitiers in 1356. The name French Row may have come from the French prisoners who were confined in one of its gabled houses after Louis VIII had brought aid to the barons in the civil war of 1216 following the signing of Magna Carta. The earliest reference to the street is in a deed of 1385, where it is called *Vicus Francorum*. The clock-tower on the left is one of the few medieval civic belfries remaining in England : its curfew bell, known as ' Gabriel,' was cast in 1355.

The great church, the western towers of which are in the background of Mr. Spurrier's light-hearted picture, was bought for the parish in 1877, when it became a cathedral. It suffered irreparable damage from the views of Lord Grimthorpe, a fanatical controversialist in ecclesiastical and architectural matters ; having contributed toward the cost of urgently needed repairs, he imposed his vandalistic ideas for restoration upon the architect, Sir Gilbert Scott.

Lord Chancellor Bacon took the title of Baron Verulam when King James I raised him to the peerage, and later became Viscount St. Albans. His mansion was at Gorhambury, just outside the town, where the local church contains a life-size monument of him in marble erected by his secretary. The poet William Cowper, during a period of his mental illness, lived at Dr. Cotton's private asylum in St. Albans. Charles Dickens knew the town well, and it is claimed locally that the original of Bleak House is here.

STEVEN SPURRIER

FRENCH ROW, ST. ALBANS

SOUTHEND is in summer the loudest and heartiest, the most crowded and uninhibited of the resorts within easy journey of London : a Cockney Coney Island, a Blackpool without Blackpool's organised grandiosity. People from London E., N.E. and S.E. swarm to it for the day, week-end or summer holiday ; drink all its beer and eat from its famous stalls most of the whelks, cockles, mussels, heaped shrimps, jellied eels and spluttering sausages ; flock to the beach for gregarious bathing or to the equally famous pier ; and, having acquired on the way paper hats (' Coming my way ? ' or ' I'm Young and Lonely '), proceed to the Pleasure Park, misnamed the Kursaal, and its Fun Fair. For those less resonant the Corporation upholds, amid shrubberies remote from the mud flats on which ships' hulks have become wooden houses with fancy names, the genteel appendage of Westcliff.

It is only in the past fifty years that Southend has become its gargantuan self : since the railway from London came, the population has jumped from under 2,000 to over 140,000. South End in the mid-eighteenth century was no more than a group of cottages at the southern end of the parish of Prittlewell, three miles from the once-flourishing port of Leigh, where in the course of a hundred years a local family called Haddock gave two Admirals and seven Post-Captains to the Navy. During the Mutiny on the Nore in 1797, the mutineers moored the ships in line from Southend to Sheerness ; and their shortage of food led to many raids on farmhouses near the shore.

The first attempt to turn Southend into a pleasure-resort was in 1768, when the new fashion of sea-bathing gave promise of prosperity to coastal villages : it failed through absence of the entertainments that were offered by rival watering-places which enjoyed Royal patronage. A measure of success came in 1801 when the Prince Regent's young daughter Charlotte was sent there. In those days Southend was placid and decorous. It had a theatre, but this did not prosper, though the young Edmund Kean, on his benefit-night, declaimed as Shylock, sang as Apollo, danced on the tight-rope, set to with Belasco the pugilist and wound up as Harlequin. The houses of Royal Terrace to the right of Pier Hill are relics of that Regency period. Later the young Disraeli wrote his *Revolutionary Epick* in Southend and praised its climate : ' You could not have a softer clime or sunnier skies.'

Of the pier, at low tide stretching over a waste of brown mud to deep water, Miss Kate O'Brien wrote in 1934 : ' It is the longest pier in the British Empire and therefore, perhaps, the longest in the world, since only the English, one imagines, make a real hobby of piers.' As long ago as 1848 *Punch* referred to it as Southend's ' longest peculiarity ' and remarked : ' Instances occur daily of a husband being at one end and a wife at the other not seeing one another for hours.' An electric tramway, said to be the first of its kind in England, was installed during the 1880's along the pier's mile and a half.

SOUTHEND   *JOHN PIMLOTT*

THE CHANTRY HOUSE, HARLOW, is Elizabethan so far as concerns the main building to the left in Mr. Michael Rothenstein's picture. Its cream-plastered walls have moulds of the Tudor rose and the fleur-de-lys. Inside, the beams of oak and elm, immensely strong, indicate the basket-like framework of the house. The present owner has converted the old barn on the right into living quarters, and has joined it to the house through a connecting section. The ancient pink tiles on the roof are inhabited by a multitude of martins. The chantry on this site was founded in 1324 by John de Stainton in honour of St. Petronilla the Virgin. It was suppressed under Edward VI, when it was valued at £9 0s. 10d.

Harlow, a large village about seven miles north-east of Epping on the main Cambridge road, has literary associations. Benjamin Flower, famous (or notorious) for his violent opposition to Pitt and the French wars in the late eighteenth century, printed and published his monthly *Political Register* from Harlow between 1807 and 1811. His daughter Sarah, after a brief career on the stage, wrote poetry on social and political themes, and many anthems and hymns, among them *Nearer, my God, to Thee*, for which her equally gifted sister Eliza composed the music.

Matthew Prior, the seventeenth-century poet, after his release from two years' imprisonment on a charge of high treason, became owner of Down Hall, near Harlow, through the munificence of Lord Harley, son of the first Earl of Oxford; in an amusing ballad, he tells how he and Harley's agent passed through Harlow. Anthony Trollope, while living at Waltham Cross from 1859 to 1871, attending to his Post Office duties and writing his novels to a daily schedule, hunted from Harlow twice a week during most winters; his eyesight was poor and he records in his *Autobiography* that ' few have investigated more closely than I have done the depth, and breadth, and water-holding capacities of an Essex ditch.'

The village is doomed to replanning as one of the new ' satellite ' towns; it will provide for some sixty thousand people, including many from Tottenham, Leyton, Walthamstow and other areas of North London.

THE CHANTRY HOUSE, HARLOW

MICHAEL ROTHENSTEIN

Plate 62

THAXTED

NORMAN JANES

THAXTED, though its residents are fewer than 2,000, has one of the noblest and largest churches in England. In the Middle Ages it was a prosperous centre of the wool and cutlery trades. The church dates partly from 1340, but during the next 170 years it was much enlarged, particularly by aisles wider than the nave and by a finely proportioned chancel, believed to have been finished under the direction of Edward IV, whose royal arms are sculptured on the north porch. The spacious interior makes an instant appeal to the eye, with its elegant white stonework and magnificent timbered roofs.

Edward IV's mother, daughter of the first Earl of Westmorland, was Lady of the Manor about 1480, when the three-storey, timber-framed Guild or Moot Hall (its twin gables are among the housetops just below the church-tower) was built by the local Cutlers' Guild. Fine old houses of the 15th, 16th and 17th centuries grace the streets. In one of them was born in 1575 Samuel Purchas, who inherited many of Hakluyt's manuscripts and based on them 'a history of the world in sea-voyages and land-travels.'

Thaxted and its church were much in the news during the 1920's when the so-called ' Red Vicar,' the Rev. Conrad Noel, promoted and extended his Christian Socialist ideas with such actions as hanging in his church the red flag of the Workers' International, inscribed with the words ' He hath made of one blood all nations.' Part of the Press denounced him, and forceful reaction came from Cambridge undergraduates and others. But Conrad Noel aimed to make his church the centre of community life, as in past ages ; he introduced colourful fabrics into the building, drew crowds with ancient ceremonial and with music according to the old English tradition (helped during the 1914-1918 war by Gustav Holst, who was then living in the parish and composed *The Planets* here) and revitalised the religion not only of his parishioners but of pilgrims from further afield. He justified the mixing of religion with politics by maintaining that ' politics, in the wider sense of social justice, are part and parcel of the gospel of Christ.' His son-in-law, the Rev. Jack Putterill, formerly his curate, carries on the tradition.

HIGH WYCOMBE, THE LITTLE MARKET HALL : High Wycombe evoked from William Cobbett the comment, 'A very fine and clean market-town ; the people all looking extremely well ; the girls somewhat larger-featured and larger-boned than in Sussex and not so fresh-coloured and bright-eyed.' Its present main street, along the valley of the Wye, is the bugbear of Oxford-London traffic, as no by-passing is possible for five miles.

The well-proportioned church in its centre is the largest in Buckinghamshire. It was originally built by the Abbess of Godstow about 1274, but the tower was erected in 1522 by the vicar, one Roland Messenger, who was as zealous at tower-building as he was at the burning of heretics : Cardinal Wolsey chose him to supervise the building of the tower of Christ Church, Oxford. A stained-glass window given by Dame Frances Dove (founder of Wycombe Abbey School for girls) in memory of famous women depicts, among the Saints, Elizabeth Fry, Florence Nightingale, Christina Rossetti, and Mary Slessor, the West African missionary.

Below the church in Mr. Fairclough's sketch is the octagonal Little Market Hall, with leaded roof and lantern, designed by the Adam brothers in 1761. Once the Town Clerk's office, it is now a club for aged and unemployed men. Hucksters of old clothes and much else set up their stalls beneath its arches.

A few steps along the High Street to the right is the Red Lion Hotel, from the portico of which a foppish young man, with black hair trained in ringlets, harangued an election crowd in 1832. 'When the poll is declared,' he ended, pointing to the tail of the scarlet lion that stands above the street, 'my opponents will be *there* : and I '—pointing to its head—' shall be *here*.' But neither then nor later did Wycombe send Disraeli to Parliament.

High Wycombe's main industries are the manufacture of paper and chairs. Local mills for paper-making opened in the seventeenth century, and white paper was manufactured which Defoe said was excellent for newspaper-printing. In 1787 the Gold Medal of the Royal Society of Arts was awarded to John Bates, who invented a method of producing paper suitable for mezzotints and other engraved plates. Chair-making, carried on by individuals called ' bodgers ' amid the local beech-woods, developed in the Victorian century to such an extent that the Council of the small town proclaimed the manufacture, for all purposes and occasions (St. Paul's and the Crystal Palace were among the customers), of chairs by the hundred thousand—chairs, in fact, at the rate of a chair a minute all the year round.

W. FAIRCLOUGH

HIGH WYCOMBE, THE LITTLE MARKET HALL

WEST WYCOMBE

W. FAIRCLOUGH

WEST WYCOMBE, founded in the eighth century A.D., was bought entire by the Royal Society of Arts in 1929, after conferences under the presidency of two Prime Ministers (Mr. Stanley Baldwin and Mr. Ramsay MacDonald) had recorded the urgent need to preserve Britain's ancient cottages and houses. The Society collected a fund of some £15,000, reconditioned the village, and in 1934 handed it over to the National Trust. Sir John Dashwood later added to the gift the neighbouring Church Hill and his beautiful eighteenth-century manor-house and park, laid out by the famous landscape-gardener Humphry Repton.

The spick-and-span High Street presents a history of rural architecture in microcosm : five centuries are represented, and black-and-white Tudor adjoins elegant Georgian in unstudied harmony. On the right of Mr. Fairclough's picture is the fifteenth-century Church Loft, once a hostelry kept by the monks of Bisham Abbey for pilgrims to a nearby shrine. Its long upper room contains a wooden reading-desk fixed to the outer wall, and a chamber for the machinery of the seventeenth-century clock that overhangs the road. A shallow cross carved in the last vertical timber-post marks the position of the crucifix that hung (till John Hampden's Puritans removed it) over the block of stone on the extreme right, with scooped-out surface bearing witness to the travellers who knelt a moment in prayer. On the left of the archway the iron stanchion of a whipping-post is still in position. The archway leads to a grassy hill crowned by the Church of St. Lawrence, standing on the site of a thirteenth-century church within a circular Iron Age earthwork.

The donor of the church was the Sir Francis Dashwood who became Lord Le Despenser and Chancellor of the Exchequer under George II, but who had been the main begetter of the Hell Fire Club. The twenty-four 'Knights of St. Francis' in that odd association were so named after himself (they included Frederick Prince of Wales and the demagogue-democrat John Wilkes, who later denounced the club and did much to enforce its dissolution). The sportive pseudo-mysticism of the Hell Fire Club spread from its headquarters at Medmenham Abbey, near Marlow, into the church at West Wycombe and the caves on the hillside. Though the ceremonial has been loosely characterised as a form of Satanism, it had Paphian aspects (the motto being 'Love and Friendship') which affected many young women of the district. Mr. H. J. Massingham invokes the recurrence of doves in the decorative *motif* on the church's font and ceiling, and the snake curling up the tripod of the font, as evidence that the ceremonial was a revival of the fertility-rites in the old Greco-Oriental worship of Kybele, Rhea and Aphrodite.

Another weird reminder of Sir Francis Dashwood is the family mausoleum which he erected next to the church. Open to the sky, it is a hexagon of high flint walls containing more than forty round-headed arches ; funerary urns in their niches contribute an impression of fantasy.

SHELLEY'S HOUSE, WEST STREET, MARLOW : In 1817 Shelley took a twenty-one year lease of the pseudo-Gothic Albion House and moved into it with Mary Godwin (whom he had recently made his legal wife), their son William, Byron's illegitimate daughter Allegra and the latter's mother, Claire Clairmont. He entertained many guests, including the Leigh Hunts, William Godwin, Thomas Hogg and Thomas Love Peacock. Tirelessly he walked in the woods, visited every place of interest within sixteen miles, rowed or sailed on the river and distributed to the cottagers soup and medical advice. It was in Albion House that he wrote *The Revolt of Islam*, and Mary Godwin wrote *Frankenstein*. But Marlow's river-mists did not suit him, the house was let, and in February 1818 the *ménage* moved to London. The richer residents of Marlow considered Shelley a madman. In the cottages the memory of his good works remained for many years. Peacock, who had found Albion House for the Shelleys, himself lived in Marlow, and in July 1818 he wrote to Shelley : ' I have changed my habitation, having been literally besieged out of the other by horses and children.'

Many fine Georgian houses adorn West Street and High Street. On the river bank, by the suspension-bridge, stands the spired parish church. Its curiosities include a neglected painting of ' The Spotted Negro Boy '—an eight-year-old albino child from the Caribbean, with brown-splotched skin, who died in Marlow in 1812 after being exhibited to the public. It also has a stone relief displaying a four-horsed coach with broken wheel, erected by Parliament to commemorate the accident on Holborn Hill which in 1632 killed Sir Miles Hobart, the M.P. for Marlow, who had been imprisoned in the Tower by Charles I for locking the door of the House of Commons on the day when Members held the Speaker down in his chair while resolutions were passed against the King's attitude on religious questions.

Marlow's Catholic Church of St. Peter, built by Pugin, preserves a strange relic : a small blackened and embalmed left-hand, severed at the wrist. Tradition claims it as the hand of St. James the Apostle, which was brought to England by Henry I's daughter, the Empress Matilda, and given to the Benedictine Abbey of Reading. The hand disappeared during the Dissolution under Henry VIII, but in 1786 the present relic was found in a walled-up box among the ruins of Reading Abbey : from Reading's museum it passed into Catholic possession, and was later presented to St. Peter's Church.

SHELLEY'S HOUSE, WEST STREET, MARLOW

W. FAIRCLOUGH

BEACONSFIELD : THE CHURCH AND THE SARACEN'S HEAD. The small town of Beaconsfield is divided by the main London–Oxford road. It is famous for its old inns and attractive Georgian houses, and for having given its name to Benjamin Disraeli when Queen Victoria made him an earl : his estate was at Hughenden, five miles away.

The church is the burial-place of the Caroline poet Edmund Waller and of Edmund Burke, the eighteenth century's great orator. Waller, a King's man in opposition to his cousin John Hampden, retired to Hall Barn, his estate near Beaconsfield, after years of exile in France following his complicity in the Royalist plot of 1643. His ornate tomb is surmounted by an obelisk resting on marble skulls. Hall Barn was bought in 1881 by the first Lord Burnham, owner of the *Daily Telegraph*. Edward VII was his guest there each year from 1892 until his reign ended. The Waller family had also owned Gregories, a farmhouse and estate which Edmund Burke purchased in 1768 and which in the twentieth century became the home of J. L. Garvin, famous as editor of the *Observer* for thirty-five years.

Another notable inhabitant for twenty-seven years was G. K. Chesterton, who wrote in his *Autobiography* : ' I have lived in Beaconsfield from the time when it was almost a village to the time when, as the enemy profanely says, it is a suburb.' His house Top Meadow, where he died in 1936, had a stage that served as his dining-room.

The half-timbered Saracen's Head hotel, with a structure believed to contain ship's timber from the *Mayflower*, is said to have derived its name from an episode in 1194, when Richard Coeur-de-Lion, returning from the Third Crusade, drank freely at this inn ' untille ye hedde of ye Kinge did swimme ryghte royallie,' after which he began to lay about him with his battle-axe. A courtier remarked that he wished the King had the head of a Saracen before him as ' he would play ye duce wyth itte,' whereupon the sobered King paid for the damage and granted permission for the house to be called Ye Royal Saracen's Head. The Emperor Charles V stayed there in 1522 ; so, in 1616, did Charles I on his way to Berkhamsted. The present lounge was at one time used as a police-court, the prisoners being brought from the old lock-up at Aylesbury End.

The Plate opposite is from a water-colour by Frances Macdonald.

R ADNAGE CHURCH: The small but scattered parish of Radnage in Buckinghamshire, numbering some 400 people and lying along a wooded valley below Bledlow Ridge, has an ancient church and a remarkable rector. The position of the church, commanding a wide view of the valley but remote from anything big enough to be called a village, comes from the fact that it was built on the site of a Celtic burying-ground and probably of some temple. The tiny window near the base of the Norman tower in Mr. John Piper's picture is the only remnant of the Saxon period in the fabric, though the interior has an unusual Saxon font. Thirteenth-century mural paintings, including a head of St. Christopher and a Tree of Life, have been uncovered and restored by Professor Tristram; and rare consecration crosses are incised on the tower's eastern arch where the nave goes through it.

The church has been altered at various dates through the centuries: three different roofs can be traced; the present one dates from the fifteenth century. The interior owes much to the skilful work of the present rector, who with the help of a few villagers constructed most of the fittings and rescued the building from its previous dilapidated condition.

In the adjacent Rectory, a large, rambling Elizabethan house, the Rev. B. J. Corder has lived for forty years. His parishioners, until the 1920's, scarcely suspected that the two attic rooms which he had turned into laboratories were the scene of potent discoveries. This quiet and unassuming rector of a hamlet in Buckinghamshire is a scientist of international reputation. He was one of the first experimenters in wireless; he invented a mine-detector which was developed on a large scale by the French Government; and in 1925 he demonstrated on a transatlantic line his apparatus for speeding up the transmission of a number of messages simultaneously on the same cable. Already in the 1890's he was demonstrating that electrical waves emanated from the human body, and he has detected such emanations from the protoplasm of a hen's egg. He also took part in cancer research in association with the late Sir Ronald Ross.

The Plate opposite is from a water-colour by John Piper.

HOME COUNTIES: WESTWARD

THE LONDON APPRENTICE, ISLEWORTH, gets its name from the apprentices of the old City Companies, who made a practice of coming for a day's enjoyment on the Thames in what were completely rural surroundings. There have been inns on the spot for about 600 years; the present building dates from the late seventeenth century but has Victorian accretions. Highwaymen who frequented the Bath Road and Hounslow Heath used it as a rendezvous; so did smugglers, who slipped up and down river with the tide. The inn's long dining-room on the first floor, decorated with Hogarth's prints of the Industrious and Idle Apprentices, has a wide built-out window overlooking Kew Observatory across the Thames and the island known as Isleworth Ait. Between here and Kew the Roman armies crossed the river under Julius Caesar in 54 B.C. and Appius Claudius in A.D. 43. The motor-cruiser *Rapid I*, which rescued hundreds from Dunkirk in 1940, is moored below, in what at low tide is a mud flat.

The bars of the inn are warm and intimate, especially on winter evenings. Generations of artists have frequented the inn, including Turner (who painted in the district when he was a schoolboy in Brentford) and, probably, Richard Wilson, Constable and Cotman. In most years a new picture of The London Apprentice appears in the Royal Academy or some other London Gallery. The road to the right of the picture bounds the park-meadows of Syon House. The original Syon House was a great nunnery of the Daughters of Sion. Henry VIII imprisoned Catherine Howard in it before she was beheaded. The present Syon House, remodelled by the brothers Adam in the eighteenth century, was built by Lord Protector Somerset. After his execution it was given to John Dudley, Duke of Northumberland, father-in-law of Lady Jane Grey; and in it the Crown was forced on this hapless victim of a dynastic plot before she was carried by barge to be proclaimed Queen in the Tower of London, where she died on the scaffold. Syon House later became the seat of the Dukes of Northumberland of the Percy family, who still own it.

Given that Isleworth is only eight miles from Hyde Park Corner, it is remarkable that the open country just south of The London Apprentice is so rich in birds: the raucous cry of the heron is heard often; so are the clacking of wild duck, the hum of flying swans and the spring chorus of song-birds; and owls hoot nightly.

Plate 68 opposite is from a water-colour by Adrian Bury.

KEW GREEN, just north of Kew Gardens, has for three centuries been a place of quiet and unusually pleasant residence. In this it resembles other corners of the borough of Richmond that are within twelve miles of London (Richmond Green, Petersham and Ham Common) as well as Strand-on-the-Green, over Kew Bridge on the Middlesex side of the Thames. All these benefited from nearness to the old royal palace of Richmond and the later royal houses within Kew Gardens : the White House, demolished in 1802, and the Dutch House, still existing, which together formed a palace for the Hanoverians.

The number of George III's children increased yearly, and since they could not all be accommodated in the palace, the houses round Kew Green became the homes of surplus royalty, their preceptors and Court officials. Ernest, Duke of Cumberland, Augustus, Duke of Sussex, and the Princess Elizabeth were moved out to King's Cottage on the Green, while William, Duke of Clarence, and Edward, Duke of Kent, went to Cambridge Cottage, on the south side (now the Museum of British Forestry, which has been incorporated in Kew Gardens). The Duke of Cumberland, following his marriage, moved into Church House, later called Hanover House when he became King of Hanover (this stands about fifty yards left of the row shown in the picture).

The Green was packed with people and carriages on the days when Kew and Richmond Gardens were opened by George III, who made a point of showing himself and his many offspring to the public as an example of family life. After his attempted assassination by a mad housemaid in 1786, Kew expressed fervent sympathy and such loud huzzas when it next saw the King that (as Fanny Burney recorded) : ' This testimony of loyal satisfaction in the King's safe return . . . affected the Queen to tears : nor were they shed alone ; for almost everybody's flowed that witnessed the scene. The Queen, in speaking of it afterwards, said, " I shall always love little Kew for this !" '

Kew Green was noted for its cricket-matches in the eighteenth century. Frederick, Prince of Wales, in 1737 played against a team captained by the Duke of Marlborough, a large sum of money being wagered on the match. ' Smock races,' run by scantily clad women, were popular, smocks being given as prizes. Rowlandson depicted a military review on the Green.

Many artists have favoured Kew Green. Sir Peter Lely lived there in Stuart times ; Gainsborough and Zoffany are buried in the churchyard of St. Anne's Chapel, the parish church on the south side. The Duke of Teck proposed in Kew Gardens to Princess Mary of Cambridge, who married him in this church ; and in her young days their daughter, Queen Mary, often stayed with her grandmother at Cambridge Cottage.

The iron gates of Kew Gardens fronting the Green were erected in 1846 to the design of Decimus Burton, who was also responsible for the great Palm House and the Temperate House when the Gardens had become famous as the home of rare plants and flowers from all over the world.

The Plate opposite is from a water-colour by Rupert Shephard.

RICHMOND BRIDGE : 'No place like it,' wrote Disraeli of Richmond. And certainly, England in summer offers few views more pleasing than this of the Thames, the bridge and the Terrace on Richmond Hill.

On June 10, 1814, while Napoleon was at Elba and Europe had relaxed in false security, a procession of visiting Allied royalties and generals, including the Emperor of Russia and the King of Prussia, stopped for an hour-and-a-half at the top of Richmond Hill on their way to Ascot Races. 'All expressed themselves,' reported *The Times*, ' quite delighted and in rapture with the well-known and exquisite beauty of a scene, which all foreigners have pronounced unsurpassed in Europe.' After descending the hill, the procession, by the postilion's error, split up, the Emperor being driven leftward to Kingston while the Prussians crossed Richmond Bridge.

Before 1777 only an ancient ferry connected the Surrey and Middlesex shores; then the elegant bridge (painted by Turner and Constable) was built with money raised on tontine shares (a system whereby an annuity was shared between subscribers to a loan, the shares increasing as subscribers died, so that the last survivor obtained the whole amount). Tolls were imposed until 1859, when the last surviving shareholder died.

Small craft of all kinds—canoes, rowing-boats, punts, sailing dinghies, motor launches—collect on this part of the Thames ; and on summer evenings the croon of the gramophone floats loud to the land. In the 1840's, to quote Mr. Arthur Bryant's *English Saga*, ' the well-to-do merchant and shopkeeper, arrayed in top-hat, white tie and long tail-coat, would sit in a punt of a Saturday afternoon perched on a chair with rod and line, dining afterwards at the Star and Garter and calling on his way home at the pastrycook's to buy his wife six-pennyworth of Maids of Honour '—the latter being a special kind of cheesecake which was still made in the town up to the 1939-1945 war. The Star and Garter, a famous resort for well-to-do Londoners until the early twentieth century (it was the background for a scene in Shaw's *The Doctor's Dilemma*), has disappeared in favour of the Star and Garter Home for men badly wounded.

There have been river festivities at Richmond since Tudor times, when processions of State barges made their way to London. The grassy bank on the left of the picture belonged to the garden of the former Richmond Palace, built by Henry VII in 1499, after a fire had destroyed the previous structure.

Catherine of Aragon, first wife of Henry VIII, gave birth to her short-lived son in Richmond Palace, and Queen Mary Tudor and Philip of Spain spent part of their honeymoon there. Queen Elizabeth was imprisoned in the palace for a brief period by Mary ; and, long later, she died there. The baby Prince James, later to be known as the Old Pretender, was nursed through an early illness in the same palace : when, in 1688, James II and his second wife drove to Richmond to see him the *London Gazette* reported that ' his Majesty was pleased to order that the Breast should be given to him, which hath (God be thanked) succeeded very well to the great joy of their Majesties.'

RICHMOND BRIDGE   *JOHN PIMLOTT*

MEAR'S FERRY, TWICKENHAM: This ferry crosses the Thames just north of Eel Pie Island, a river resort since the days of Henry VIII, who is said to have visited the island to eat the eel pies of one Mistress Mayo. Twickenham, now best known for its football ground where international Rugger matches are played, is still the most pleasant of Middlesex suburbs, though its heyday was in the eighteenth century when a part of Society came to live

> Where silver Thames round Twit'nam meads
> Her winding current swiftly leads ;
> Twit'nam, the Muses' favourite seat,
> Twit'nam, the Graces' loved retreat.

Horace Walpole, who wrote these lines, bought in 1747 a Twickenham villa (originally a cottage built fifty years earlier by the Earl of Bradford's coachman) and made it the core of his fantastic ' Gothic ' castle, Strawberry Hill. He justified his erection of battlements by a text from Deuteronomy. The former castle is now a Catholic training college. Of the equally famous villa of the poet Alexander Pope, who was in Twickenham visited by Voltaire, Swift and John Gay (then writing *The Beggar's Opera*), nothing remains but the ' grotto ' under the road dividing the estate.

Pope was buried in the churchyard of St. Mary's, to the right of the picture. He set up a plain tablet to his dead parents and his living self on the wall of the church's north gallery ; his own verses, ' For one who would not be buried in Westminster Abbey,' are inscribed nearby on a triangular plaque devised later by Bishop Warburton. A tablet on the outside wall commemorates ' the moral virtues ' and ' well-earned fame ' of the actress Kitty Clive.

Below the church, a winding lane to the right leads past the site of Orleans House, which was bought in 1800 by the Duc d'Orléans (later King Louis-Philippe), who passed two periods of exile in Twickenham and gathered round him a little colony of Bourbon minor royalties.

James II received York House, an imposing mansion on the London road behind St. Mary's, from his father-in-law, Lord Clarendon. James's daughters Mary and Anne, both future Queens of England, were born in it. York House was bought by the Twickenham Borough Council in 1924 for use as the town hall. Its grounds include fountains dominated by late nineteenth-century statues of nymphs much more than life-size, which epitomise all that is exaggerated in the Victorian conception of well-fleshed nudity and bosomry. Further along the lane, past Twickenham Ferry, lies Marble Hill Park, which makes the foreground of the famous panorama from Richmond Hill across the river. Its great house was erected by George II for his mistress Mrs. Howard, afterwards Countess of Suffolk ; Pope was the ' contriver ' of its gardens ; and Dean Swift humorously described himself as ' chief butler and keeper of the ice-house '—a deep well in which blocks of ice cut from the frozen Thames could be kept in storage (this ' ice-house ' was used as an air-raid shelter in the 1939-1945 war). Later, the house was rented by Mrs. Fitzherbert, and in it she was married to the Prince Regent.

MEAR'S FERRY, TWICKENHAM

EDWARD WALKER

HIGH STREET, GODALMING, freed by the Guildford by-pass from the Portsmouth Road's traffic, has recaptured much of its charm as an old market-highway. The Regency building in the centre (it is shown without its pillared cupola, removed in 1946 for repair or replacement) was erected on the site of the Market Hall where a local Hundred Court sat in session. Until modern municipal offices were opened, it served as Town Hall and Police Court. Godalming in the nineteenth century was the first town in England to instal electric lighting in the streets ; and in the twentieth, it is unique in having converted the old Town Hall into a combination of public convenience on the ground floor and museum on the first floor. The gabled, timber house on the left used to be the White Hart Inn : it has an abnormally high archway, built to give room for the piled-up waggons of wool. Weavers, mostly from Flanders, settled in Godalming during the fourteenth century, and the trade in wool and cloth was extensive when Queen Elizabeth granted the town a charter.

Peter the Great of Russia stayed in 1698 at the King's Arms in the High Street with a large retinue, whose gluttonous bills of fare are preserved in the Bodleian Library at Oxford. Alexander of Russia and Frederick William of Prussia also dined there in 1814. Near the railway station lies the manor of Westbrook, which belonged to General James Edward Oglethorpe, the philanthropist who in 1733 founded in America the colony of Georgia, governed it with distinction and repelled a Spanish attempt to conquer it. A contemporary engraving in the museum shows him at the sale of Dr. Johnson's library in 1785—a tall old man with jutting chin, reading small print without spectacles.

The town's present industries include tanning and paper-making (the mills date from James I's reign), flour-mills and timber yards and market-gardening. Sir Osbert Sitwell recalls, in *The Scarlet Tree*, the second volume of his autobiography, how in his childhood he used to be taken driving from his grandmother's house at Gosden to the nursery gardens at Godalming : ' Here were lines of long, narrow hothouses, filled in mid-winter with row after row of Edwardian magnates' buttonholes ; red and crimson carnations that seemed already in their fragrance to hold a hint of the aroma of cedar-wood boxes and cigar-smoke that was to be their ultimate destiny. . . .'

Much custom, too, has come from Charterhouse School, which migrated from the City of London in 1872 to Victorian-Gothic buildings on a nearby hill-top : its striking chapel was designed by Sir Giles Scott as a war memorial to Old Carthusians.

HIGH STREET, GODALMING   W. E. NARRAWAY

Plate 73

WINDSOR CASTLE AND OLD BANK HOUSE

VINCENT LINES

HOPS and heresy, like fruit and vegetables, became widespread under Henry VIII ; and it was in his reign that an ancient family named Aldem founded a brewing and private banking business in the royal borough of Windsor. The present Old Bank House is close to the site of the Aldems' manor-house : the brewing association remains in Courage's offices on the ground floor.

William the Conqueror, who liked hunting in the local forest, began the castle, and the work was continued by his Norman successors ; parts of Henry II's building still stand. The Plantagenet kings often used Windsor Castle as a prison for distinguished captives : the Dukes of Orleans and Bourbon after Agincourt, King John of France, Kings David of Scotland and James I of Scotland, who first saw his bride, Lady Joan Beaufort, as she walked in the gardens below his room. Edward III, who was born at Windsor, lived in the Round Tower (top left in the picture), which was altered for him by William of Wykeham, who is said to have occupied the Winchester Tower next to it ; and in 1347-1348 Edward III founded the Order of the Garter in the St. George's Chapel. The Emperor Sigismund, on becoming a Companion of the Order in 1416, brought with him to Windsor the supposed heart of St. George, which was preserved in the castle until Henry VIII's time.

The Castle, now nearly a mile in circumference, was extended or altered or reconstructed or neglected according to the outlook of the day's monarch. It was the summer residence of Charles II, who appointed Wren to be its Surveyor-General, and of Queen Anne. Fanny Burney describes George III walking on the famous terrace with his many children, and setting an example of family life to his subjects. The royal castle was extravagantly run under George IV and William IV. Albert, as Prince Consort, undertaking one of his first State tasks for Queen Victoria, cut out the extravagance : he is said to have discovered the castle servants holding, when royalty was absent, a fancy-dress ball in which a ' Queen ' and a ' Consort ' postured. The low posts and chains bordering the road on the left surround Sir Edwin Lutyens' simple memorial to George V, bearing the inscription : ' First Sovereign of the House of Windsor.'

THE JOLLY FARMER, FARNHAM, is an inn of Elizabethan structure, refaced in Victorian times. It stands opposite the bridge on the south side of the River Wey. William Cobbett, the stalwart egalitarian of *Rural Rides* and *The Political Register*, champion of country life and disliker of London as the ' great wen,' was born here in 1762, a son of the innkeeper. As a lad he worked on his father's farm and at Farnham Castle. ' When I first trudged afield,' he writes, ' with my wooden bottle and my satchel over my shoulder, I was hardly able to climb the gates and stiles.' Cobbett ran away from home at the age of eleven to see Kew Gardens ; he reached Richmond with only threepence in his pocket, and spent it on a copy of Jonathan Swift's *Tale of a Tub*, which ' produced what I have always considered a sort of birth of intellect.' He was buried, after a very vigorous life, in a heavy, solid tomb near the door of Farnham Church.

Farnham, since Cobbett's day, has expanded from a small town into a fair-sized one, and beyond that into an adjunct of Aldershot. It has been for centuries a centre for agricultural produce : Defoe records that in his day it was the largest corn-market in England ' except Hampstead and London.' The castle, built by Henry of Blois, Bishop of Winchester, in about 1142, owed its importance to the ancient Tin Road near by, later known as the Pilgrims' Way. It now looks down on a group of beautiful Georgian houses in the fine, wide Castle Street.

Craftsmanship in the making of implements was for long a tradition in the town. The late George Sturt (author of *A Small Boy in the 'Sixties*) and his ancestors worked as wheelwrights in East Street for two centuries ; in *The Wheelwright's Shop* he gives an excellent account of the wheelwrights' craft before the coming of the machine-age.

Farnham, with its neighbouring parishes, was a cradle of cricket in the South of England during the late eighteenth century and the early nineteenth. Cricketing residents included Harry Hall, the gingerbread-baker who preached the doctrine of the straight bat and the left elbow up, and William Beldham (' Silver Billy '), champion batsman of his day, whose bat, hanging in the old man's cottage kitchen, inspired the Rev. John Mitford (editor of the works of English poets and himself a notable cricketer) to write : ' Reader ! Believe me when I tell you I trembled when I touched it ; it seemed an act of profaneness, of violation. I pressed it to my lips and returned it to its Sanctuary.'

THE JOLLY FARMER, FARNHAM

BARBARA JONES

BOULTER'S LOCK, MAIDENHEAD

W. FAIRCLOUGH

BOULTERS LOCK, MAIDENHEAD : Boulters is probably not a proper name, but derives from the miller's term 'boulting' : there had been a water mill here for several centuries before the lock was built in 1772, just after the regulation of the flow of the Thames had been undertaken by Act of Parliament. Richard Ray, the first lock-keeper, received a house and a wage of 6*s*. a week, with an extra 4*s*. 6*d*. for driving and taking care of the Navigation Commissioner's barge-horses, which were kept for towing. Boulters was rebuilt in 1912, and later obtained an electric boat-conveyor, the only one of its kind on the river.

On Ascot Sunday in Edwardian and neo-Georgian times, the lock was crowded for most of the day by launches and punts with coloured cargoes, from the house-parties around, of ladies in picture-hats and long, resplendent dresses, of men in white flannels and straw boaters ringed with Old School colours, of picnic-baskets and cases of champagne.

A short way downstream is the stone bridge carrying the Bath Road into Maidenhead. It was built in 1772 by Sir Robert Taylor, a stonemason's son who became Sheriff of London and prospered so greatly as an architect that he was able to leave £180,000 to the University of Oxford for the teaching of European languages. His bequest permitted the Taylorian Institute to be erected as the headquarters of the University's linguistic studies.

A wooden bridge had existed here for centuries. For its upkeep a guild was incorporated in Maidenhead in 1352 ; the bridge was held by the Earl of Kent against Henry IV in 1400, and for James II in 1688 by an Irish regiment whom the local inhabitants put to flight by a ruse.

Close by, toward Bray, is the younger Brunel's railway bridge, painted by J. M. W. Turner ; it is said to have the widest brick arches in the world, and it was duplicated when the Great Western Railway doubled the track.

TARRY STONE HOUSE, COOKHAM : Cookham lies on the Cliveden reach of the Thames, one of the loveliest of the river's stretches, with the woods on Viscount Astor's estate sloping steeply to the water's edge. The road on the right of the picture was until the nineteenth century part of the main Oxford–London route, which turned to the left into Mill Lane, just beyond the houses in the middle distance.

The Tarry Stone (left) formerly marked the boundary of the Abbot of Cirencester's grounds ; in the Middle Ages it was a racing mark for the village sports which took place on the Feast of the Assumption. It spent some time in a private garden, and was restored to the parish in 1909 by Sir George Young, who had been an administrator in Gladstone's Governments. His great-grandfather, Admiral Sir George Young, the first Treasurer to the Board of Commissioners of the Thames Navigation (later the Thames Conservancy), had a mansion at Cookham, Formosa Place, which was built largely by his sailors, in the shape of his quarters on the poop of a warship.

Tarry Stone House dates in part from Queen Anne's reign but the existing façade was added early in the nineteenth century. In the late nineteen-twenties it was bought by the John Lewis Partnership ; and under the name of the Odney Club it is one of a group of houses comprising a country club where workers in the various shops of the Partnership can go on holiday with their families. Further down Ferry Lane, to the left of the picture, is Lullebrook Manor, under the same ownership.

The parish church is of Norman foundation. Among its memorials is a tablet to Captain Roger Ashwell Pocock, founder of the Legion of Frontiersmen, and others of the same family. An earlier Pocock buried here is the painter Isaac, who, after inheriting property at Maidenhead in 1818, became a successful writer of melodrama and adapted some of the Waverley novels as operas. Two distinguished modern painters, the brothers Stanley and Gilbert Spencer, were born in Cookham ; the former has used Cookham backgrounds for his highly individual pictures of Biblical and other subjects.

TARRY STONE HOUSE, COOKHAM

W. FAIRCLOUGH

THE GUILDHALL AND MARKET CROSS, WINDSOR : The Guildhall, to the right of the water-colour, was begun in 1686 from the design of Sir Thomas Fitz, Surveyor of the Cinque Ports, and was finished in 1689 under the direction of Sir Christopher Wren, whose father had been Dean of Windsor. As with many local Guildhalls, the ground floor was open to the street and was used as a Corn Exchange. To quieten Corporation doubts about the strength of the structure, Wren inserted four pillars beneath the main room ; but in fact there is a gap of several inches between their tops and the floor they were supposed to uphold.

Wren also presented the statue of Queen Anne's consort, Prince George of Denmark, clad in Roman armour and wearing an eighteenth-century wig, which adorns a niche at the south end of the Guildhall. The statue of Anne herself, seen in the picture on the building's first-floor level, was erected by the Corporation at a cost of £40 and was originally painted and gilded. Below it is a fulsome inscription in Latin, the translation of which reads : ' Sculptor, Anne cannot be copied by your art. Do you wish to carve Anne's likeness ? Then carve a goddess.'

Market Cross House (centred in the picture), now a coal-merchant's office, bears the date 1687. The Market Cross, taken down in 1691, was probably at the junction of the four roads where Queen Victoria's statue now stands ; it was the subject of a petition to Charles I, accusing Godfrey Goodman, Bishop of Gloucester and Canon of Windsor, of having ' re-edified and repaired ' it and of having set upon it two coloured religious pictures savouring of Popery.

The two-storeyed inn in the background, the Carpenter's Arms, has been built on the site of a much older tavern. Behind it lies the house in Church Street where Nell Gwyn is said to have lived. Near-by, where the Queen's Mews now stands, was Burford House, assigned to her by Charles II. Wood's pharmacy, on the left, was established in 1770.

This part of Windsor town was several times visited by plague, and as early as 1563 Queen Elizabeth decreed instant hanging for anyone found arriving in Windsor from London at a time when there was plague in the Capital. In the Civil War Windsor was on the Parliamentary side, it being said that all Berkshire was loyal to the King, ' save only that barren division of Windsor.' The Corporation blacksmith, however, continued to work at the castle but refused to accept ' the usurper's ' money and wore a hat without a crown ' until there should be a crowned head again in England.'

The Plate opposite is from a water-colour by Vincent Lines.

UP-RIVER: THE VIEW FROM THE WINDSOR-ETON BRIDGE.

The view is upstream, looking toward the bend of the Thames that curves round to Brocas meadow, named after the Brocas family who were long connected with Windsor and Eton (a Sir Bernard Brocas was beheaded for conspiracy against Henry IV). The landing-stages and buildings beyond the Bridge House Hotel comprise the Eton College Boathouse. Queen's Ait, the island headquarters of the Queen's Ait Club for ' wet bobs ' of the College, is four and a half miles upstream; there is frequent traffic to it on fine summer afternoons in ' whiffs,' ' perfects,' pairs, fours and ordinary rowing-boats. Just over a quarter-mile downstream is Fellows Ait, where the Eton Procession of Boats, led by the ten-oared *Monarch*, is held on the Fourth of June.

Windsor, beyond its association with Castle and College, is a Middle Thames port from which river excursions run upstream to Maidenhead, Cliveden, Cookham, Marlow and Oxford, or downstream to Staines, Kingston and Magna Carta's Runnymede Island. Boveney, where the famous Kit-cat Club of seventeenth and early eighteenth century celebrities met at Downs Place, home of the bookseller-publisher Jacob Tonson, is just beyond Brocas round the bend. Swan-upping, the process of marking for identification the swans belonging to the Dyers' and Vintners' Companies (all unmarked swans are the property of the Crown) takes place at Romney Lock, a little way downstream from the bridge.

The Bridge House Hotel in the picture incorporates part of a much older inn, the Catherine Wheel: this latter a common sign used in the past by innkeepers who promised safety for travellers (the name was borrowed from the Knights of St. Catherine of Mount Sinai, vowed to the protection of pilgrims journeying to the Holy Sepulchre). Opposite Bridge House is the Old House, now an hotel, which was built and for a while inhabited by Sir Christopher Wren.

A bridge existed at least as early as Windsor Castle. Two mills at Eton were recorded in Domesday Book. The main highway to London crossed the river here in the Plantagenet era, though the Court usually came by barge from London to Datchet ferry. In 1276 the poor inhabitants of Windsor petitioned Edward I to allow them to take pontage for eight years to repair and amend the bridge. Thereafter, there was unceasing friction between the authorities and people over tolls. The latter were still collected throughout the nineteenth century, both for passing over (a corpse cost 6*s*. 8*d*.) and passing under. Joseph Taylor, an inhabitant of Eton, undertook to free the bridge from what he considered a very unjust imposition; his struggle against the Corporation began in 1895, and final judgment was given for him three years later. He celebrated his success in a pamphlet that versified :—

> ' The Task is o'er, the work is done.
> The Gate is lost, the Bridge is won.'

The Plate opposite is from a water-colour by Vincent Lines.

SECTION VIII

HOME COUNTIES: SOUTHWARD

THE WHITE HART, BROMLEY: This historic hotel, facing a modern shopping-street, has records going as far back as 1509, when the owner, Robert Beckyngham, bequeathed the property to endow a school at Guildford; a document states that the Mayor and five approved men of that town rented it to Andrewe Broome for £12 a year ' to the use of the Scholemaster and Usher of the free grammar schole in Guldeford.' King Edward VI's Grammar School still receives this rental. There exist two copper tokens which were issued as currency at a time of shortage of small change; they are stamped with a hart and with the names of two successive landlords of the hostelry, the later being Thomas Ghost, 1664. The citizens of Bromley organised in 1792 an association that declared its loyalty to the Crown and protested against the revolutionary doctrines then seeping over from France; a book containing their Declaration was displayed for a fortnight in the White Hart, where it obtained 326 signatures.

The inn-front originally extended to the roadway, in line with the buildings on either side; but with the growth of Bromley as a residential area for London merchants, and its importance as a posting-house for coaches on the London-Hastings road, the need for a forecourt induced the occupier, William Pawley, to pull down the old building in 1828 and erect a new one (which he called Pawley's Family Hotel) some thirty feet back from the roadway. The inn must have been very prosperous then, for it was said that it could stable a hundred horses; and four coaches a day were plying between Bromley and London. Pawley promoted an annual flower-show in the hotel's garden and race-meetings on Bromley Common, and was a cricket enthusiast: in 1844 he engaged John Lillywhite (son of the famous cricketer) as groundsman of the White Hart field. The latter was noted as an umpire: his no-balling of Willsher at the Oval for bowling with his hand above his shoulder resulted (in 1864) in overhand bowling being officially authorised. It was on the White Hart field that the historic single-wicket match between the two greatest cricketers of the day, Alfred Mynn and Nicholas Felix (whose real name was Wanostrocht), took place in 1846: a picture of the event is in Lord's pavilion.

On the wedding-day of Edward Prince of Wales and Princess Alexandra in 1863, a carrier called Nesbit consumed in public, in front of the White Hart, a vast pie labelled ' All for Me ' and consisting of 5 lb. of rumpsteak, 4 lb. of flour, 1 lb. of lard, and four of the largest potatoes obtainable: all this and a half-gallon of ale too.

Plate 79 opposite is from a water-colour by Lilian Goodchild.

Dover i 1810 roku

DOVER, FROM WELLINGTON BRIDGE : 'Dost thou know Dover?' asks Gloucester in *King Lear*. Few travelled Englishmen in the last several centuries have not known it. Its white cliffs are the symbol of return to England, as witness Kipling's

> How stands the old Lord Warden?
> Are Dover's cliffs still white?

The Lord Warden (no longer an hotel) is on the harbour front below the cliffs that face the track of the cross-Channel steamers. Wellington Dock is in the foreground of the picture ; and one end of Snargate Street, a relic of the old town of Dover, is on the left. In August 55 B.C. Julius Cæsar had been able to sail right up the inlet between the hills shown to right and left : he recorded that ' the forces of Britain drawn up in arms on the hills ' made him retire ; and he chose an easier place further up the coast for his successful landing later.

' Dover ' is the first word in the Domesday Survey of 1086, which mentions the town's ship-service to William the Conqueror. Dover Castle, which lies outside the scope of the drawing to the right, or east, of the Connaught Barracks seen on Castle Hill in the right-hand background, dates from Norman times. The Constable of the Castle is always the Lord Warden of the Cinque Ports. Famous Wardens of the past (the office is now held by Mr. Winston Churchill) include William Pitt the Younger and the Duke of Wellington : during the latter's Wardenship, kit marked ' Private William Pitt ' was found in the Castle, testifying to Pitt's enthusiasm for the local volunteers, known as the Cinque Port Fencibles, with whom he occasionally drilled when Napoleon was threatening the country from the French coast.

The Western Heights were first fortified during the American War of Independence, but the Drop Redoubt on the left of the picture was begun in preparation against Napoleon's expected invasion. Three staircases (known as the Grand Shaft) are cut into the cliff near the Redoubt, being labelled ' Soldiers,' ' Officers and Ladies ' and ' Women.' Caves near the Shaft could shelter about 2,000 people during the 1939–1945 war, when German guns on the French coast subjected Dover to regular bombardment. It was from Dover on St. George's Day, 1918, that Admiral Sir Roger Keyes sailed for the famous raid on Zeebrugge.

Dover pilots, now under Trinity House, formed one of the oldest guilds, the need for them being caused by the difficulties of the Dover Passage. In 1656 the crossing by packet-boat took John Evelyn seven hours, and a second voyage in the same year took eleven hours ; he was very sick and the boat was chased by pirates. The first steam-packet to make the crossing was the *Rob Roy* in 1820, and in 1830 the *Firefly* (considered then to be the wonder of the age) crossed in three hours.

The Plate opposite is from a water-colour by Randolph Schwabe.

THE MILL HOUSE, FARNINGHAM: About five miles south of Dartford, Farningham lies on the hill below the main arterial road between London and Maidstone. The pleasant High Street, with its weatherboard houses, descends to the bridge over the River Darent, next to which, opposite the Lion Hotel, is the entrance to the Mill House. Corn-mills have stood on the site since the time of Domesday Book.

The present mill, one of the finest of its kind surviving in England, was rebuilt in the 1790's with Canadian timber. It has an unusual and elegant mansard (two-stage) roof at the base of which perch ornamental eagles in lead. A 'lookum' projecting from the upper storey formerly held the winch for hauling up the grain sacks. The mill ceased to be economic at the end of the nineteenth century, and later the first floor was converted into one large living room. The adjacent house of grey brick obtained its two pairs of graceful bow-windows when the Mill was rebuilt, but its back portion may date from Elizabethan times. The adjoining river, before being polluted shortly before 1914, was famous for its trout : a model of the largest fish taken serves as weather-vane to the cottage on the left of the picture.

Farningham manor-house, damaged by bombs in 1941, lies just beyond the bridge. Captain William Bligh, R.N., central figure of the mutiny in the *Bounty* in 1789, lived in it quietly toward the end of his life, brooding over his forcible deposition from the Governorship of New South Wales and his two years of Australian imprisonment (though on his return to England he had been vindicated, and promoted in 1814 to be Vice-Admiral of the Blue).

In Farningham churchyard a massive marble mausoleum holds the remains of Thomas Nash, the wealthy Lambeth J.P. and calico-printer whose legacy of £1,000 on his death in 1778 may have helped his nephew John Nash (then a pupil in the office of Sir Robert Taylor) to strike out independently along the road to great performance in the rebuilding of London and Brighton.

THE MILL HOUSE, FARNINGHAM

RANDOLPH SCHWABE

BIDDENDEN, an attractive village some four miles from Tenterden, is characteristic of the Kentish farming country ; but until the eighteenth century it was one of the minor centres of the Kentish cloth industry, Cranbrook being the chief. In 1565–1566 six persons from Biddenden were fined in London for offences in connection with the cloth trade ; and one Roger Pattenson, a Yorkshireman, is recorded as a prominent clothier of the village in the early seventeenth century. In the picture the row of red-brick houses with dormer windows under one red roof, beyond the cream weatherboard Chequers Inn on the left, was once a single dormitory-building for clothworkers. The wide village street has pavements of slabbed marble, each 15 feet wide.

The village was famous in the sixteenth century as the home of the Siamese twins Eliza and Mary Chulkhurst, who were joined together at the hips and shoulders. One was taken ill and died at the age of thirty-four ; the other refused an operation to be separated, and died six hours later. They bequeathed their local land to provide an annual distribution at Easter of loaves and cheese to five hundred poor people : a charity still undertaken by the trustees of the fund. Until the recent war it was customary to distribute a form of biscuit stamped with a representation of 'The Maids,' and visitors crowded to Biddenden for the ceremony. Local belief had it that a girl who preserved her biscuit unbroken until the Midsummer Eve in the same year would be married before the following Easter.

Vincent Lines

BIDDENDEN

CANTERBURY has a documented history of 1,300 years. Beyond that, it was for at least four centuries a Roman town called Durovernum, standing at the point where four roads from the Kentish ports converged to form a great thoroughfare leading to the Thames crossing at Londinium. Excavations that were begun by German bombs in 1942 and 1944 (they destroyed the cathedral library) have uncovered new Roman material.

It was about A.D. 600 that Canterbury became the mother-city of the Church of England. St. Augustine, arriving from Rome with forty monks in 597, was welcomed by King Ethelbert, and became the first archbishop of a cathedral which grew out of an existing church. After suffering from fire and pillage in pre-Norman wars 'the Great Church' was rebuilt and enlarged under the Normans by Archbishops Lanfranc and Anselm; some of their work remains in the tall cathedral that dominates the small city, but after their time fire brought further disaster; much of the structure was rebuilt in the fourteenth century's Perpendicular style, to the designs of Henry Yevele, Edward III's master-mason. The splendid central tower contains a bell that tolls only for the death of a King of England or an Archbishop of Canterbury.

Canterbury's most resonant event in history was the murder in the cathedral of Archbishop Thomas Becket, by the four knights who thought they were fulfilling the will of Henry II. The Church gained from the deed a martyr's tomb before which Henry prostrated himself in penance, and to which during the following centuries pilgrims journeyed from all parts of the country—lordly and lowly, as Chaucer has immortalised them. Henry III was present in 1220 at the installation of Becket's bones in a costly shrine. When this was demolished in 1538 at Henry VIII's command, two huge chests were needed for packing the gold and jewels, and twenty-six carts for removing the rest of the treasure. Near the empty space in St. Thomas's Chapel where the shrine of Becket once stood (known as the Martyrdom) are the tombs of the Black Prince and his nephew Henry IV.

Other distinctive buildings are scattered round Canterbury: King's School, partly occupying the ancient monastery within the cathedral precincts and claiming descent from a sixth-century monastic school—its scholars have included Christopher Marlowe, William Harvey (discoverer of the circulation of the blood), Walter Pater, Sir Hugh Walpole and Mr. Somerset Maugham; the remains of St. Augustine's Abbey; some famous churches; the city wall and West Gate; and many medieval houses.

'Canterbury Week,' in early August, attracts thousands to the cricket matches and theatrical productions. Members of I Zingari flaunt their club colours; and the Old Stagers who claim to be the oldest existing amateur dramatic society, perform to packed houses. The Fountain Hotel, traditional headquarters of the Old Stagers, disappeared in the grievous destruction that came to Canterbury in the second World War.

Plate 84

BRIGHTON FRONT is more than a promenade : it is a boulevard in the grand manner, a period-piece blending the Regency and the Edwardian with oddly harmonious effect.

As a place of assembly it is more entertaining, because more variegated, than Hyde Park's Rotten Row ever was. Mr. Rushbury's picture, which looks toward decorous Hove, has bow-fronted Regency in the foreground and, further back, a sequence of opulent large hotels which, in Edwardian and neo-Georgian times, were a home from home for the hearty rich from the Board Rooms, the Turf and the Stock Exchange, the stars of the music-hall and of musical comedy, the spenders, the ' knuts ' and the ' good-time girls.' Beyond the traffic on the left and above the shingled beach is a broad, concrete promenade where, on any Sunday morning at any time of the year, polite crowds of all sorts breathe deeply and parade in wide lines of fashion and near-fashion : brisk youth and ambling age, uniforms and loose flannels, tweeds and satins, invalid chairs and baby-carriages.

So it has been in Brighton ever since the late eighteenth century. First, Dr. Richard Russell proclaimed that the sea-water of Brighthelmstone should be *drunk* for glandular health ; and before very long the place itself became known as ' Dr. Brighton.' Next, the Prince of Wales, having first visited the new resort to annoy his father, George III, made it his second home. He installed Mrs. Fitzherbert in the Pavilion ; the bucks and beauties and sports followed him ; John Nash and other architects developed graceful squares and the modish quarter called the Steyne. The notable and notorious persons of the Regency period were visitors—Fanny Burney, Sheridan and Byron among them. Jane Austen wrote in *Pride and Prejudice* : ' In Lydia's imagination a visit to Brighton comprised every possibility of earthly happiness. She saw, with the creative eye of fancy, the streets of the gay bathing-place covered with officers.'

The Prince Consort patronised Brighton ; so did Macaulay, Thackeray and Gladstone : but neither they nor the nineteenth century itself could make it decorous. Disraeli and Dickens (who wrote *Oliver Twist* there) did not try.

THE FRONT, BRIGHTON

HENRY RUSHBURY, R.A.

BRIGHTON : A WET DAY.   Rain does not deter the crowd from enjoyment at Brighton.   Its theatres have a metropolitan standard ; and the Palace Pier in the picture has an amusement hall, a concert hall, a dance-floor, restaurants and shops.   Beyond it is the famous aquarium, in which the collection of living marine creatures rivals that of Monaco.   This pier was built in the 1890's to supersede the old chain pier, erected in George IV's reign, where Queen Victoria embarked on State visits to the Continent when Brighton was a main port for cross-Channel ships.

In the middle distance the Queen's Hotel projects into the roadway : its near corner was the site of the celebrated vapour baths of Saki Dun Mahomed, the East India Company's surgeon who introduced shampoos and vapour cleanings to England (he died in 1851 at the age of 102).   Round the bend is the Royal York and Albion Hotel, formerly the residence of the ' wicked ' Duke of Cumberland.   It was acquired in 1913 by Sir Harry Preston, Mayor of Brighton, benefactor of local hospitals and Regency figure born out of his time : a dapper little Corinthian who attracted to his hostelry hundreds of the English celebrities of the 1920's, from the then Prince of Wales to the latest prize-heavyweight, by way of Lord Lonsdale, famous lawyers, novelists, politicians, actors, jockeys and a broad-minded bishop or two.

Further beyond the bend is the old port, above which there stands on a slope a surviving part of the old village of Brighthelmstone, which originated when William the Conqueror leased the place to his son-in-law at the price of 4,000 herrings a year.   The young Charles II, six weeks after the Battle of Worcester, escaped to the Continent from Brighthelmstone.   The resort's sea-bathing began in this area during the eighteenth century, when men (including George III) bathed stark naked.   The habit persisted in lesser degree for half a century : Mr. Arthur Bryant quotes in his *English Saga* a French swimmer at Brighton who, when completely nude, saw to his horror a mother and two pretty daughters on camp-stools between him and his bathing machine, each holding a prayer-book.   ' To give them a hint without offending their modesty, I advanced cautiously on all fours, raising myself by degrees as much as decency permitted.'

Brighton has obtained many eulogies.   William Cobbett said that it surpassed in beauty all other towns in the world.   A more charming extravagance was that from the Secretary to the first Chinese Ambassador (the year is 1877, the translation is by Mr. Arthur Waley and the quotation is from *Brighton*, by Osbert Sitwell and Margaret Barton) : ' I was quick to admire its matchless beauty . . . . I have visited famous places in many lands ; but never on any day has Pu-lai-tun been absent from my thoughts, such power does this place hold over all who have beheld it.'   At the other extreme comes this from Dr. Johnson, at his most bearish after he had stayed with Mr. and Mrs. Thrale in West Street :   ' So truly desolate that if one had a mind to hang oneself from desperation on being obliged to live there, it would be difficult to find a tree on which to fasten the rope.'

BRIGHTON: A WET DAY   *NORMAN JANES*

THE OLD MARKET HOUSE, STEYNING   *RANDOLPH SCHWABE*

OLD MARKET HOUSE, STEYNING : The small town of Steyning, characteristic of southern Sussex, lies close to the northern entrance to the gap in the South Downs through which the River Adur flows to its outlet at Shoreham. Its origins are in the mists of early Christian legend. The story goes that St. Cuthman miraculously prevented his father's sheep from straying by drawing a circle round them with his crook. Later, on setting out for his travels, he fashioned a sort of wheelbarrow in which he pulled his aged mother by a rope. The rope broke, so he twisted twigs of elder to serve instead. When haymakers mocked at him a sudden storm ruined their crop, leaving Cuthman and his mother untouched. Cuthman vowed to build a church wherever the new rope should break ; so at Steyning the church was founded, and St. Cuthman himself was buried in it.

Ethelwulf, King of the West Saxons and Kentishmen, was also buried here in 858, though his body was later removed to Winchester. Alfred the Great, his fifth and best-loved son, had estates in the neighbourhood. Steyning was a port in Saxon times, the river being navigable up to Bramber near-by, from which a creek extended to Steyning. At the time of Domesday Book it was one of the largest towns in England.

Edward the Confessor gave lands at Steyning to the Abbey of Fécamp, whence came the monks who built the town's first Norman church (the present church dates from the twelfth century). King Harold deprived Fécamp of these lands, thereby giving Duke William one of his excuses for invading England. After the Conquest the Abbots of Fécamp had wide powers in Steyning, outside the orbit of the English Archbishops ; and these persisted till Edward I ended the French sway by his law forbidding aliens to hold property in England.

Steyning has other links with religious history. In 1555, during the persecution of Protestants under Queen Mary, John Launder, one of the Sussex Martyrs, was arrested in the town and burned at the stake. A hundred years later George Fox, founder of the Society of Friends, preached in the market-place at a time when nonconformists were suffering persecution.

Professor Schwabe's picture shows a stretch of the High Street with houses dating from various periods. The building with the clock is the Old Market House, with a steeple containing the town's fire bell. The old industry of fell-mongering, the treating of animal skins, chiefly Sussex sheep ('fell' being hide with the hair on it), is still carried on locally. At Steyning's former cattle-fair between two and three thousand animals were often sold in a day.

FISHER STREET, LEWES, before 1622 was called Fish Street and was a market for the Brighthelmstone fishwives. It is a turning off the High Street, which with its byways has many attractive buildings from different periods. Among them is the Bull House carved with the figures of satyrs; it was occupied in the 1770's by a Quaker tobacconist whose daughter married his lodger Tom Paine, then an excise officer and later the revolutionary friend of the new American republic, who wrote the *Rights of Man*. At the corner of a lane leading from the High Street to Lewes Castle stands the fine old Barbican House. The Town Hall is on the site of an inn before which Richard Woodman, a Protestant farmer, was burned at the stake with nine other men of Sussex during the heresy-hunting inspired by Mary Tudor.

Visitors flock to Lewes for various reasons: its status as the county town of Sussex, its historical interest, its many schools in the country around and the Races on the bracing course on top of the South Downs. Lewes has also become the nearest English equivalent to Salzburg: music-lovers from all over the country gather in it for Mr. John Christie's summer festival of opera, superbly produced in the private theatre at Glyndebourne, his mansion two miles outside the town. Lewes also prides itself on its torchlight procession of 'Bonfire Boys' on Guy Fawkes' Night.

Lewes was in 1264 the scene of an early victory for constitutional government over despotism, when Simon de Montfort and his party ('democrats before an age of democracy,' to quote Professor G. M. Trevelyan) defeated and captured Henry III, winning the battle 'with prayer, psalm-singing and cold steel.' The Castle has well-preserved remains, the pride of which is the early fourteenth-century barbican, three storeys high, erected as a strongly fortified gatehouse and guarding the drawbridge over the moat. In the garden entrance to the Castle grounds is a five-spike section of the iron railings which were made from Sussex charcoal-iron to encircle St. Paul's Cathedral (against Sir Christopher Wren's wishes) and were taken from the cathedral in 1874.

The churches of Lewes are rich in legend and notable architecture. St. Anne's has an anchorite's cell, in which a thirteenth-century woman lived by her open grave until her death; her remains were discovered when the cell was opened seven hundred years later. Southover's church contains the grave of William the Conqueror's fifth daughter, Gundrada, and her husband Earl William de Warenne; the lead coffins containing their bodies came to light when excavations for the railway-line to Lewes were made on the site of their Priory of St. Pancras, which survived until Thomas Cromwell destroyed it at Henry VIII's orders.

FISHER STREET, LEWES

DOROTHY WATTS

ARUNDEL : The view is northward from the River Arun, across meadows to coloured roofs that are dominated by the vast Roman Catholic church of St. Philip Neri, built in the mid-nineteenth century for the fifteenth Duke of Norfolk by Joseph Hansom (who designed the hansom cab as well as grandiose buildings in the Gothic style). The great church, so large that it is filled only at the Christmas Midnight Mass and the Feast of Corpus Christi, has become a magnet for Catholics : in particular for the local families which for generations have served the FitzAlan-Howards at Arundel Castle, the ancient seat of the Dukes of Norfolk, Hereditary Earl Marshals of England and Premier Peers of the Realm. About one-third of the population of Arundel are Catholics ; though these include few of the tradesmen.

Right of the picture, on the brow of the hill, is the parish church of St. Nicholas. The chancel arch of this church is blocked by a brick wall which separates it completely from the eastern part of the building, where lie the splendid FitzAlan-Howard tombs dating from the fifteenth century. A quarrel between the Protestant Vicar of St. Nicholas and the Catholic Duke of Norfolk ended in a law-suit in 1879, when Lord Chief Justice Coleridge decided that the FitzAlan Chapel was the private property of the Norfolk family. Thus one edifice contains the Protestant parish church and the Roman Catholic ducal chapel, which is now within the Castle precincts.

Arundel Castle stands high above the Arun bridge, beyond the right of the picture. Turner and Constable painted its immensity and splendour. The early owners of the castle styled themselves ' Lords of Arundel,' until an Act of Henry VI confirmed that possession carried with it the Earldom of Arundel. From 1243 twelve successive FitzAlans held sway. Then Philip Howard, eldest son of the fourth Duke of Norfolk of the Howard line, succeeded to the property and title through his mother. The Roman Catholic Duke, who had schemed to marry Mary Queen of Scots, was executed by Queen Elizabeth for plotting a Spanish invasion of England. Philip Howard himself was committed to the Tower, where he died ; and Arundel became forfeited to the Queen. The Earldom of Arundel was restored by James I to Philip's son Thomas, the first notable English collector of works of art ; he was a convert to Protestantism and was created Earl Marshal. During the Civil War the great castle was captured by the Parliamentarians and recaptured by the Royalists before it finally surrendered to Cromwell's Sir William Waller.

The Dukedom of Norfolk was given back to the Howards by Charles II in 1660 ; but it was not until the early eighteenth century that Arundel Castle again became the family's principal seat. The family own and ably administer 20,000 acres of good Sussex land. West Sussex, mostly rural, is fortunate in its two large-scale landlords, inheritors of a benevolently feudal outlook ; the other being the Earl of Leconfield, who gave the vast but well-proportioned Petworth House (some eight miles to the north) to the nation in 1947.

The Plate opposite is from a painting by Oliver Hill.

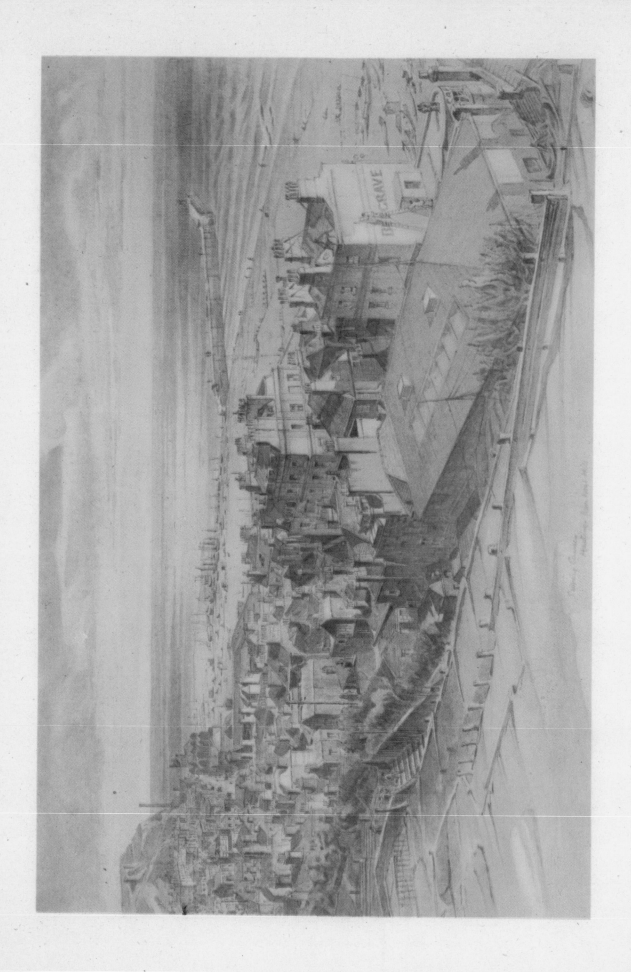

HASTINGS: The main part of the town has become an average resort for the respectable though gregarious; but the old town to the east, here sketched by Mr. Causer, is a medley of interesting narrow streets, with the fishing quarter known as the Stade, below cliffs that contain caves formerly used by smugglers.

On the shore stand the curious tall black wooden net-houses in which the fishermen store their gear and dry their nets. Hastings fishing-boats are immortalised by J. M. W. Turner in a picture which he left to the National Gallery on condition that it should always hang close to a similar painting by Claude. Up a valley running inland from the Stade are two of Hastings' old churches: All Saints', with its celebrated fifteenth-century 'Doom' painting above the chancel arch (Titus Oates, who fabricated the Popish Plot, was curate of this church in 1674, while his father was vicar), and St. Clement's, where Dante Gabriel Rossetti was married in 1860 to the beautiful but ailing Elizabeth Siddal, who died from an overdose of laudanum two years later.

Hastings—the name derives from the Saxon tribe of Haestingas—first appears in history in the tenth century. It then (like Steyning) became associated with the Abbey of Fécamp in Normandy, of which the wife of King Ethelred the Unready was patron. Partly because of local Norman influence, William the Conqueror chose Hastings as the landing-place for his invasion, but wind and tide carried him instead to Pevensey, and the actual battlefield of 1066 is seven miles inland. On Hastings Hill a castle was erected which the Norman family of Eu held till 1248; it was the headquarters of one of the 'rapes' or districts into which the Normans divided Sussex.

In medieval times Hastings was a notable Cinque Port, but its trade gradually passed to Winchelsea and Rye owing to the loss of its Norman harbour through coast erosion, and to destructive raids by the French. Queen Elizabeth granted the town a Charter in 1589, when it was prominent as a fishing centre. John Collier, several times Mayor in the first half of the eighteenth century, developed the town's amenities, but it was not until the nineteenth century that Hastings became a fashionable resort. By that time two gems of Georgian architecture, Pelham Crescent and Wellington Square (named after the Iron Duke, who as a Major-General had commanded the new barracks), had been built, and the Brighton-Hastings railway was opened.

Charles Lamb complained: 'There is no sense of home at Hastings. It is a place of fugitive resort, an heterogeneous assemblage of sea-mews and stock-brokers, Amphitrites of the town, and misses that coquet with the Ocean.' Other literary lions rated the place more highly. Byron, Leigh Hunt, Crabbe, Rossetti, Carlyle, Coventry Patmore, Dickens and Thackeray stayed in Hastings for long or short periods.

The Plate opposite is from a water-colour by Sidney Causer.